D1506704

Apotheosis Now

Rabbit Hole to the Beyond

Yanhao Huang

CONTENTS

CHAPTER ONE: TRANSFORM- ATION

ENTER THE RABBIT HOLE

Do you want happiness or success? When most people hear this question, they think: of course, it's happiness! Because the ultimate purpose of success is happiness, right? Otherwise, why do we even want success at all? And yet, many times in our life, we have achieved success in various forms —like a new job or a new relationship—but happiness continues to elude us. Whenever we reach a goal, we may be happy for a short while, but happiness always seems to subside again, as we are soon off struggling to reach a new goal.

For some people who have contemplated the question a little deeper, the question itself may be problematic because it assumes that happiness and success are mutually exclusive—why can't we have both? There are certainly people who seem to be happy and successful, as they are not only conventionally successful but that they are also successful at being happy. For most of us, however, success seems to come at an expense to our happiness. We believe that only from our constant dissatisfaction with life will we have the necessary drive to endure the hardships that will eventually lead us to success.

Therefore, most of us continue to grind our way through life. We are starting to become tired of all this striving and achieving because no matter what we do, our happiness is still nowhere in sight. We are even beginning to forget what happiness is like because happiness is rarely present and alive. Instead, it has turned into an idea, a memory, and therefore dead. Similar to love for many people, we don't even know if happiness is a real thing. It is only when we are suffering greatly that we start to ask the more profound questions of life, like: "What is the meaning of life? What is the nature of existence? Who am I? How do I get what I want? What do I even want? Is there a God? What is the truth?"

You may have opened this book because you want those questions answered, so you can gain some knowledge to improve your life in some way. This book will address such questions; however, the primary purpose of this book is not to give you any more new knowledge. Instead, it aims to break the existing belief system you have built to unveil a much greater intelligence that's already within you, so this intelligence can flourish and operate over your life.

Now you may ask, why should I relinquish control of my life? I thought I had a system to keep my life in order while directing it in a certain way, and I should learn something from this book to manage it better? Reflect on all the things you think you did so far. Did they really bring you lasting happiness? Or are they merely psychological fulfillment on a conceptual level? Or, in other words, mental concepts to indicate the progress you made in life? Like in the aspect of career, possessions, relationships, or whatever else you have measured yourself against others.

In this game of life, all milestones can only bring you temporary satisfaction; all past progress is hollow as they are just memories; you depend on validation from external sources constantly to sustain their fleeting reality. Internally, you always feel the same; your core is still empty despite all the achievements and pleasures you have tried to fill it up with. The spontaneous joy that was so pervasive in your childhood only occurs in brief moments when your life conditions have finally aligned with your expectations, before they quickly diverge again when your conditions or expectations change.

For those who have gotten far ahead in this game of life, you may begin to realize that it is fundamentally unwinnable and can only bring you more suffering the more you play, for those who are behind also suffer, except they are more likely to think that more success can solve their suffering.

Nevertheless, most of you cannot give up this game because the rules of the game—or the hierarchical system, in other words—are constantly being reinforced in your psyche by society throughout your life. Your sense of self is heavily derived from standing somewhere on this ladder. Being above certain others has become the primary meaning of your life. What you may not notice is that this ladder is actually more like a wheel —as no matter how much progress you think you have made—you are never there. Even if you have made it to the "top," you are still bound by time and will eventually fall, while constantly being threatened by another to surpass you. Thus, your position is never secure and you are often in a state of unease as a result. You may think you need this pain to drive you to achieve more and so you can finally reach permanent happiness. On the contrary, this pain not only takes the joy out of your life but can also hinder your success by causing you to do the wrong things.

If you examine your life closely, you can see that the best things you achieved depended on many factors that were beyond your control. If you study the stories of the world's most successful people— even the ones who were considered to be mostly self-made—you can see that the most significant contributing factors to their successes were beyond their control—like someone gave them a shot or their product had the right timing, and so on. Nothing can materialize without the universe's co-operation.

Going a step further, even all the things you think you did were not done by you. Your thoughts, actions, and whatever else you think you are doing are a product of a chemical process that's happening within your body. The same process that is sustaining your life right now without you doing a single thing. The most important event of your life was your birth which you had absolutely no control over.

We are not separate entities that are independent of our environment; we can only exist in the context of the whole. You may think that there are things you can control while the rest is beyond your control and is left up to luck, the universe, God, or whatever you want to call it. The reality is that this distinction between what is you and what is not you is just a mental concept. There are no individual wills. There is only a unitary process.

This book will attempt to use language to bring about an evolution in your psyche, such that your energy can start to cooperate with the universal energy rather than competing against it—and have life work for you rather than against you. If what you have read so far resonated with you on some level and you are starting to see that there may be another way to play this game of life, then you may be at that stage of transformation. If not, this book may plant a seed within you that can sprout at a later time.

WHAT IS THE "YOU" THAT CAN BE TRANSFORMED?

Teachings in the form of self-help or religious doctrine typically try to transform you by molding you into a certain person, like getting you to adopt a set of beliefs and behaviors. Such teachings can try to be as authoritative or as convincing as they like, but all external sources will inevitably pose a conflict between what the sources say and what the individual inwardly is. And this conflict will cause splits within the individual's psyche, as one part of his mind is trying to be like what the teaching says while another part is judging and correcting his behavior.

The self-help teachers actually need people's internal conflicts, whether they know it or not, because it's the divided mind that needs help; a mind that is whole will not—which will render their teachings useless. There are psychotherapists who get resistant when their patient is actually getting better, because the loss of their patient's dependence threatens their role as the helper. When some psychotherapists start to see their patient improve —they will introduce new things for the patient to address—so the dynamic between the helper and the helpee can be persisted.

Psycho-Cybernetics by Maxwell Maltz was considered to be one of the best self-help books ever written. The book can be essentially summarized by the following quote: "The 'self-image' is the key to human personality and human behavior. Change the self image and you change the personality and the behavior."[1] Although there is truth to that statement—because one's self-image does dictate one's life circumstances—but the advice still introduces the conflict between you and the self-image. Which one are you? Are you the self-image or something else? And all the problems start here because the self-help teachings do not address this fundamental question: who is the "you" who can change the self-image? If the one in control doesn't have a problem, then why do we bother changing the self-image? And if the one who can change the self-image is problematic, then how can changing the self-image help? And it is this contradiction that causes people—who try to improve themselves—to fail.

People do not see that the one who is making

the improvement is the same one who needs to be improved. When people try to improve themselves, what they really do is try to become someone based on their own projection of what this improved version is supposed to be. They do not question how their own mind—which needs improvement—can properly judge what is considered to be "improving."

People may think that there are objective metrics to judge a person's progress, but such metrics will always be subjective because no matter what kind of metrics they use, it will always be they themselves who chose it. And when people finally become this "improved person" that they have imagined themselves to be, this new version is really constructed from the same mind that they were aiming to improve in the first place—and they can never get out of this double bind. Thus, people may achieve some improvements based on their own metrics, but their psychological core remains the same.

The polarity between the existing and the improved will prevail as long as the person desires to be something other than what they are, as they will always act with another layer of agenda rather than acting for its own sake. And this disparity will manifest itself through the person's energy in the forms of phoniness, hesitativeness, and mechanicalness—which can be easily detected by others —and so will always bound the person to their existing life circumstances.

Are we not our mind? Why do we separate ourselves from it? If our mind is fearful and selfish, and out of our fearfulness and selfishness—we succeeded in becoming better than others in whatever aspects that we have measured ourselves against them—is that really improvement? Our mind would still be fearful and selfish, and even if we try to become the opposite of our mind—like selfless—but is that true selflessness? Or is it an idea of selflessness constructed from a mind that is selfish?

Now, you may be wondering, how can I actually be transformed? It seems that neither the desire to change nor external help can really do this. And this is partially true; both the desire and outside help is only effective up to a point. At best, they can guide you to arrive at something that already exists within yourself so that you can discover rather than adopt. Adopting any belief is a superficial transformation at most, because all beliefs and principles can be changed with time—and they should be since what works in one circumstance will not work in another. However, realizations on what already exists can never be changed and taken away. What is existentially real will work in all circumstances. Ultimately, you still need to come to the realization yourself, because no absolute truth can be transferred.

Information can only act as a representation of reality but not substitute it. Even a simple instruction like "put your hand on your head" is inherently vague. If you say this to a thousand people, you will get a thousand ways of putting a hand on the head. And a simple concept like a point—which mathematics has defined as a location with no length and no width—is inherently contradictory. If a point has no length nor width, then how can it exist? How can it have a location? A point must have some length and width—although very minimally—but it still must have them, and if it does, then how is it different from an area? What is the exact quantity of length and width that can distinguish a point from an area? Already we can see how reality is continuously getting split when trying to understand it through conceptual means. This is similar to how scientists are trying to explain the nature of existence—they have dissected everything down to an atom—and now we have quantum mechanics and string theory. We will continue having theories after theories because a theory can never substitute reality.

Intellect can only dissect, and so its vision will always be partial, but reality is always whole. "When analytic thought, the knife, is applied to experience, something is always killed in the process"[2] (Robert M. Pirsig). The whole can include the partial, but the partial cannot include the whole. Thus, reality can never be grasped by the intellect alone; only when you see the whole, can reality be revealed.

In the process of communication, the communicator must symbolize reality in the form of words and images, while the recipient must decode the communicator's symbols according to their own experience of reality. True communication is only possible if the recipient were able to decode the meaning of the symbols exactly as intended by the communicator. Therefore, if the recipient is stuck in a particular perspective, then the words —no matter how correct—will not be understood by the recipient as intended. Even if God himself has spoken, a newborn baby will not be able to understand anything. Therefore, communication cannot be forced by either party. Both parties must be on the same wavelength for proper communication to occur.

When you read this book, it is equally important to pay attention to your own interpretations of what is read, in addition to the words written. If you ingest the information fragmentarily—choosing some while discarding others, or agreeing and disagreeing to what is read—then you are not listening. Instead, you are further strengthening your own conditioning. As Shunryu Suzuki wrote in *Zen Mind, Beginner's Mind*:

> "When you listen to someone, you should give up all your preconceived ideas and your sub-

jective opinions; you should just listen to him, just observe what his way is. We put very little emphasis on right and wrong or good and bad. We just see things as they are with him, and accept them. This is how we communicate with each other. Usually when you listen to some statement, you hear it as a kind of echo of yourself. You are actually listening to your own opinion. If it agrees with your opinion you may accept it, but if it does not, you will reject it or you may not even really hear it."[3]

In this book, some things are meant to make you feel uncomfortable because it aims to shatter your cherished opinions and beliefs. Seeing your own disturbances and distortions is far more valuable than blindly agreeing with what is said or trying to grasp the concepts mentally. When you get disturbed, the uncomfortable feelings that arose as a result of having your self-image damaged is a fact —because the feelings are there—and the rationalizations that you generate to protect your self-image is an idea—because it's fabricated by your mind. Stay with the fact and not the idea.

When we are dealing with facts, then we see the real as the real and the false as the false. When the light of awareness lights up the map of life, then it's easy to know what to do in each situation. But if we are trying to find out what to do by thinking and reading up theories after theories, and philosophies after philosophies, then we are always in the realm of the abstract. When we are navigating through life with our clouded vision and our distorted concepts, then we are stumbling around in the dark and will get nowhere in the end.

When a nearby danger is pointed out to you in which you were previously unaware, then your very seeing of the danger would bring about instant action—you don't need to rationalize what to do. When you see an oncoming car, a greater intelligence will take over, and you will instantly get out of the way. You will not think because otherwise, it will be too late.

Similarly, if you have a tendency in dropping subtle hints about your accomplishments and the important people that you know so people could like you more, and this book says such behaviors are really masking underlying feelings of unworthiness—which ends up making people like you less because they can sense your phoniness. Then the recognition of your psychological structure can invoke your hidden pain—like embarrassment—and simultaneously trigger your defence mechanisms—that tries to run and hide from that pain, like thinking, "I know how great I am, I don't need to listen to this."

The very seeing of your defence mechanisms and painful feelings will dismantle your distorted psychological structures—you don't need to figure out how to get rid of it. Seeing is a much more substantial transformation compared to building up beliefs on how great you are. Do not turn away from yourself; stay with the facts and not the fiction that your defensive mechanism conjures up. Before you can know how to bring about a complete psychological transformation within yourself, first, you must know what exactly is the "you" that can be transformed. So, what is the source of one's being that determines one's life destiny?

THOUGHT

Many great teachers have recognized that one's thoughts ultimately determine one's destiny; a quote by Lao Tzu summarizes their insight nicely: "Watch your thoughts, they become your words; watch your words, they become your actions; watch your actions, they become your habits; watch your habits, they become your character; watch your character, for it becomes your destiny." It is important to note that Lao Tzu uses the word "watch," and not "control." Because most people assume that you can control your thoughts, so they focus solely on the effect of thought, and abide by famous quotes like Buddha's "all that we are is the result of what we have thought," and Marcus Aurelius' "our life is what our thoughts make it."

All of such observations are true, but if we don't know the actual source of life—that is even prior to thought—then we will get into endless confusions. Most self-improvement teachings stop on the level of thought, and many books became very successful in teaching the power of thought. Notable ones include Napoleon Hill's *Think and Grow*

Rich and Earl Nightingale's *The Strangest Secret.* The teachings became more simplified (in some ways) over the years and found their expression through the New Age movement toward the late 20th century—that centralized on the concept of the "Law of Attraction"—which was popularized by the movie *The Secret* in 2006.

Some New Age teachers go so far as to treat your mind like a Genie's lamp; they say that if you can think about what you want with enough "correctness," then they will be manifested in your life without exception as it is the "law" of the universe. "Your thoughts become things!"[4] as claimed by Mike Dooley. And the problem with people is that they are mostly thinking about what they don't want rather than what they do want, so they continuously attract unwanted circumstances in their lives.

The concept of the Law of Attraction is true to a certain degree, as we can observe that successful people tend to have beliefs that assert their capabilities and life possibilities. In contrast, people who are underachieving in life tend to have beliefs that limit themselves.

A more scientific explanation for the Law of Attraction is that all things are fundamentally just vibrations of energy (as stated by Albert Einstein's famous $E = mc^2$ equation). Thoughts and feelings are that same energy vibrating in a certain range of frequencies. One's thinking and feeling patterns will emit a frequency that will attract life circumstances in tune with that frequency. However, the teachings of Law of Attraction were ultimately unsuccessful because they were taught in various forms for centuries—from Hermeticism to quantum mysticism—but human beings' general state has not changed much. The wealth gap is getting wider and wider, poverty still exists on a global scale, and most people still live very unhappy lives.

The problem with the Law of Attraction teachings is that it assumes thought to be the source of existence, and so thought can override everything. As Rhonda Byrne wrote in *The Secret*: "thoughts are primary cause of everything, and the rest is effects from those thoughts."[5] So, she comes to conclusions like: "Food cannot cause you to put on weight, unless you *think* it can."[5]

Suppose everything in the universe can be simply gotten by merely "thinking" about it. Why doesn't everyone just listen to subliminal affirmations 24/7 until we all become billionaires? Are we just robots that can be that easily programmed by thoughts? How can we be sure that negative influences do not at all program us? Do you think that billionaires just "think" about money all day or "believe" that they are billionaires before they became one? If two teams want the exact same thing, like a championship trophy, is the team that thinks about it (or believes in it) more will get it?

People who became truly successful rarely thought about the goal at all, because all their energy was so absorbed in the process that they couldn't waste an iota of it on anything else. Those people were only interested in what they were doing moment by moment. They were not concerned about the end result like money, achievement, or recognition. Many of them were even surprised at how successful they became.

It wouldn't take much rational examination to see the numerous inconsistencies of the Law of Attraction. Still, we don't want to face that. We want to believe in the law so that we can have a sure and easy way of getting what we want. Otherwise, we are left with our meaningless lives. We are only concerned with how to get the law to work; we have practiced all sorts of methods like visualizations and affirmations, and sometimes we got what we want while other times we didn't—just like always—why doesn't it work all the time?

The New Age teachers will always answer something on the line of: "to really manifest something, you must believe already having it without the slightest doubt, have no conflicting thoughts, and have no sense of selfishness." And of course, there are some grains of truth to it here and there, but how exactly do we have no conflicting thoughts? To practice any kind of Law of Attraction is admitting that we lack something; otherwise, why practice anything at all? And how can our desires not come from selfishness? When we want something, even if it's to be more selfless, is our desire not centered on the self?

The New Age teachers will provide explanations after explanations for all the inconsistencies. Eventually, they will reiterate the same point: "if something did or did not happen, it is always your creation—via thinking—whether you know it or not." And we can never crack their logic because thought—like anything else in the universe —is a phenomenon that cannot be known through conceptual thinking. You need thought to explain thought, and it is caught in a recursive loop. We —the studier—are part of the phenomena that are being studied. So, we can never have absolute certainty on exactly how anything works, including thought.

The New Age teachers recognize the limitations in their teachings, so they teach partial truths and cater to our desires to get us to want to buy their products. Why is it that almost all Law of Attraction teachings only talk about attracting typical human desires like health, wealth, and relationships? If thought is so powerful, then why do we not use it to manifest supernatural things like a new universal law or an entirely new universe? Or how about things that even we ourselves cannot comprehend? Is it possible? Have we seen people do it? Given the wild imaginations that the billions of us may have, if anyone could have manifested such things, then the world would be in complete disarray, as one day we may have gravity, but the next day who knows what.

This book is not denying supernatural things. This book is trying to clarify what is really responsible for the workings of the universe. Thought is a process that is governed by universal laws, so thought cannot govern what governs it. If we want to be a genius like Albert Einstein, can we just "think" our way into being a genius? Actual geniuses don't even know how their mind works. Genius cannot be taught. If it can be, then there would be no such thing as geniuses because everyone would be just trained to be one. There would be no need to distinguish geniuses from non-geniuses. If we observe the New Age teachers themselves or other enlightened people who we think have "perfect" thoughts all the time, we can see that they still age, contract diseases, and die like everybody else. Thoughts cannot deny the process of life.

Therefore, we must recognize the inherent limitations of thought. Our thoughts are only derived from our memories, so thought cannot manufacture anything new. We cannot desire something that is outside the realm of our experience. If I have never tasted a lychee, then I can only desire the descriptions of lychee given by others; or desire tasting a new fruit. But I cannot desire the actual experience of tasting a lychee because I don't know what it is. Descriptions can never substitute the actual, so how can thought attract experiences from which the thought itself does not even know?

We must recognize that there is something beyond thought, prior to thought, and more intelligent than thought, that is responsible for the workings of the universe. This is why many people report breakthroughs and epiphanies when they are in a state of mental quietude. If you look around the universe—the trees, the insects—you can see that they effortlessly know how to survive, and yet they don't have the capacity to think.

At the end of the day, all teachings of the Law of Attraction essentially boil down to this: think about whatever you want, as long as you feel happy now, always, and that's it. And whatever circumstance that is best for you at any moment will happen. For such a seemingly simple task, what we end up getting is centuries after centuries of books, lectures, explanations, and methods, and yet most people still could not do it. The essential problem of all self-improvement teachings on the level of thought is that: we do not know how to actually think.

Most of us think that we are thinking our thoughts and can generate whatever thought we want all the time. A simple experiment can easily disprove this; see if you can not think of a single thought for the next ten minutes. Did it work? I suspect most of you could not do that. Now, start paying close attention to your thinking process; how exactly do you make a thought appear? Do you actually "do" something to generate them? Or do they simply appear on their own? The brain is just another organ in the body like the heart, lungs, and stomach; every other organ in your body is functioning automatically; what makes you think the brain is any different? What makes you think the brain is the controller?

> "In your body, there's no boss. You can argue that the brain is a gadget evolved by the stomach for the purposes of acquiring food. Or you can argue that the stomach is a device evolved by the brain to feed it and keep it alive. Whose game is it—the brain's or the stomach's?"[6] (Alan Watts, *Out of Your Mind*)

THE "CONTROLLER"

You may distinguish the mechanisms in your body between what is voluntary from what is involuntary, like you think that you can control the thoughts in your mind, the movement of your limbs, and the sounds of your voice. However, you also know that hair growth, digestion, and circulation are processes happening automatically without your conscious effort. This distinction actually only exists as a concept within your mind; there is no such distinction in reality.

When you examine your breathing process, you know that it is happening automatically when you're sleeping or are not aware of it. But, you can also feel like you could manually control your breathing when you want to. The line of distinction between anything in reality is ultimately arbitrary, as the Buddha said: "in the sky, there is no distinction of east and west; people create distinctions out of their own minds and then believe them to be true."

All the bodily mechanisms that you think you can control, try to see exactly how you are controlling them. You will eventually realize that you can't really explain it. When you do something like moving a limb, you kind of just do it, like it just happens and you can only observe it happening rather than "making" them happen. If you keep looking for a more baseline controller of yourself, you end up finding nothing except a pure witness. You can see that an act may sometimes be directed by a thought, but thoughts are not directed by anything, instead, they can only be observed, by you— the pure witness.

The "controller" that you think you are is constructed in the mind only. When an action happens or a decision is made, a thought appears in your mind and tells you that you performed that act or made that choice. For example, when someone asks you to pick between water or soda, a thought pops up and says water, so you answer water, then another thought comes and says you made that choice, and then more thoughts may come to provide some reasons on why you made that choice. But can you see that between the question and the answer, you were not actually involved? A thought simply popped up on its own; you did not choose the thoughts.

You may argue that you do choose your thoughts and you made the choice because of so and so, but whatever reasoning you come up with will also be supplied by your thoughts. If you say that you constructed that reasoning, then we come back to the same scenario; how did you construct that reasoning? What reasoning did you use to construct that reasoning? And this recursion can go on forever, and we will only find more thoughts, and they all pop up on their own.

Even if a lot of time was invested into making a decision, where careful consideration was given to all the possibilities, and a lot of back and forth was involved. But the end decision will still consist of a single thought, and all the previous consideration is also made up of thoughts. Whichever direction you go, there will only be thoughts. If you want to find a root decision-maker, then what you are really doing is trying to find a root cause. But the cause of any decision is infinite as all factors are interdependent. And if there is a root cause, then can you see that its very existence would negate you as the decision-maker? What are you choosing if the outcome has a preexisting cause?

> "We feel that our actions are voluntary when they follow a decision and involuntary when they happen without decision. But if a decision itself were voluntary every decision would have to be preceded by a decision to decide - An infinite regression which fortunately does not occur. Oddly enough, if we had to decide to decide, we would not be free to decide"[7] (Alan

Watts, *The Way of Zen*)

Any choice you think you have made at any time in your life is essentially based on your programming —which consists of your genetic instructions, karmic imprints, and the conditioning that you have received from your environment since birth—all of which was not determined by you. If you spend some time watching your thoughts and choices, you can see that they come and go just like the clouds in the sky. They are a process happening in the brain, just like a process happening in the atmosphere. Only that the mind has misidentified you as the cause for its own activities—and that misidentification is also a thought. The "you," the "thinker," the "controller" is the thought; there is no "thinker" apart from the thought.

The initial misidentification of you being a "controller" typically comes from an observation that your consciousness is limited to a body that is separate from everything else. And this body has some intelligence in navigating through the world. So the mind came to the conclusion that you are a separate entity and is responsible for operating this body.

After the conception of this separate entity, the thoughts arising on its behalf start to expand by engulfing more and more concepts about the entity, like one's attributes, beliefs, accomplishments, possessions, stories, goals, dreams, and preferences. Those kinds of thoughts then become more and more repetitive and start to form patterns in the mind. The thought patterns then get tangled up with different emotions and memories to form a bundle of energy patterns that gets stored in the body. This bundle of energy patterns behaves like software that operates over the body. The formation of this software is the development of the false you—the ego.

CHAPTER TWO: CONDITIONING

CONCEPTUAL-IZATION OF REALITY

The ego is what most people identify themselves as; it is what they refer to when they say "I." This ego—which is essentially just a concept of who people think they are—gets conditioned onto one's mind by society throughout their life.

When an infant enters the world, the infant does not know what he is experiencing; he simply experiences. There is no conceptualization of reality taking place in an infant's mind, so the mind does not interfere with the experience by constantly labeling, differentiating, judging, and commentating on everything. Like telling him what each thing is/does, what he likes/dislikes, should/shouldn't do, what is right/wrong, good/bad, and so on. The infant does not have the concept of a "self," so he cannot differentiate between the experiencer and what is experienced—thoughts, feelings, perceptions, sounds, and sensations. An infant is completely at one with the experience; to an infant, there is only what is.

After the child's birth, society starts to teach the child by drilling all kinds of conceptual knowledge into the child's head. Beginning with the naming of things, then classifying and differentiating the things based on their attributes, like that pretty thing you see on the ground is called a flower. That green stuff around it is called grass. Some botanical knowledge is then provided about the two to classify and differentiate them.

Conceptual knowledge is necessary for many of humanity's advancements. When we learn something, we need the knowledge to be stored in a conceptual form so that it can be communicated to avoid people re-learning the same thing from scratch every time. However, conceptual intelligence is only one dimension of intelligence. Similar to the intelligence in A.I. and machine learning technologies, conceptual intelligence can only know something through division and comparison; it can only know the concept of "me" through comparison with the concept of "others." Therefore, it can only attempt to know something by studying the components of its composition through continuous dissection, but it can never know anything in its totality. In addition, conceptual intelligence can only learn future actions from the data that it has already gathered, so without prior data, it becomes useless.

We are not machines; if we try to make conceptual intelligence the whole field of our intelligence, then we can only know reality by dividing it into parts, like me and others, order and chaos, good and bad. So naturally, we take sides as we want one side to overcome the other, like me to win over others, order to win over chaos, good to win over bad. Consequently, we become ignorant of the other side of reality and fail to see how the two sides are actually inseparable like two sides of the same coin.

When we function through our conceptual intelligence, then we can only think and act through the existing data that we have gathered about the world. Whatever data we gather, it will also be divided. Because we can only gather data through our sense organs, and our sense organs are inherently dualistic, so it will cut up reality into pieces. I can only feel something to be hot if my own body temperature is colder in comparison; I can only perceive what is to be small if my body is big in comparison; if I were a micro-organism, then the external world would appear to be entirely different.

Ultimately, no matter how much data we gather, it will always be minuscule compared to the entire universe. So, if we only function through our limited data, then we can never discover anything new. As Shunryu Suzuki said: "we should not hoard knowledge; we should be free from our knowledge."[1] If you have never tasted a lychee, then I can describe the taste using the most elaborate concepts, but they can never substitute the actual experience of tasting the lychee yourself. So, to know something new like the *you* beyond your ego—which is a concept of you—you cannot get there through more conceptual thinking.

> "When you keep your intellect dipped in this limited, fragmented, accumulative dimension of your mind, you draw conclusions about life that are completely distorted. The more people become engrossed in thought, the more joyless they become. ... The problem is just that they have enslaved their faculty of discernment to the limitations of their sense perception.
>
> But the same intellect can be sharpened if you allow it to soak in the other aspect of your mind—your awareness, chitta. If you want to reach your ultimate nature through the mind, you need to make the intellect truly discriminatory, in the ultimate sense. This does not mean dividing everything into good and bad, right and wrong ... Instead, all it means is learning to *discern the real from the illusory, what is existentially true from what is psychologically true*."[2] (Sadhguru, *Inner Engineering*)

Although only human beings can think conceptually in this universe (as far as we know), however, we can see that all other elements still possess tremendous amounts of intelligence. Like how the universe is composed from the galactic level down to the subatomic level; how the interactions of different organisms can form an ecosystem that sustains life; how ant colonies can behave like a human brain; and how every organism instinctively knows how to survive and navigate through the world. Therefore, we should recognize that conceptual intelligence can only play a limited role in our existence.

When parents start to assess their child's intelligence based on their ability to verbalize conceptual knowledge about things, the child starts to think that sounds and symbols used to represent the thing are more important than the actual thing itself. Unknowingly, the child is constructing a prison in their own mind and slowly becoming trapped within a conceptual model of reality. A symbol is never the thing. A symbol will always be an abstraction, a representation.

When one experiences a flower, there is the sight of a beautiful form. There are fragrances in the nose. There are sensations of touching the flower, and there are feelings of aliveness from being near the flower. All of this is lost when one just retreats into their mind and projects a mental symbol of a flower or verbalizes some information about the flower, like the flower's name and attributes. The actual experience of reality is a composition of various aspects of perception. You will never experience something the exact same way twice as reality is alive, always changing, but a symbol representing reality is dead.

When one develops the habit of conceptual thinking, they will continuously try to make sense of their experience by turning it into abstractions. Thus, they cannot see reality as it actually is and can only see its distortions through the filter of their mind. We can observe this happening all over society, as most people are mistaking the symbols for reality. They worship mental abstractions like the numbers in their bank account, the number of people they slept with, the likes on their social media pictures, their job title, and their accomplishments, thinking that it is a happy life, not knowing that it is only a representation of a happy life according to *their* conceptual model of reality. When in actuality, such symbols had only brought them psychological fulfillment by checking off some boxes in their mind, which ends up being a hollow and fleeting experience.

In people's actual day to day experience, their job with a fancy title may be stressing them out; their promiscuity may be causing a disturbance in their physical and emotional well-being; their multiple houses and cars are giving them a hard time to manage even though they can only experience one at a time; trying to get more views and likes on their social media pictures are ruining the experience of whatever they are doing in those pictures. Also, when people don't think they compare favourably to others on such symbols, they get depressed even though their actual life circumstances may be quite good. This is why we see people in affluent societies resorting to pills and drugs to maintain some sense of mental sanity and pleasantness. "What we have forgotten is that thoughts and words are *conventions*, and that it is fatal to take conventions too seriously."[3] (Alan Watts)

You are not your Linkedin and Facebook profile; when you live for your job titles and vacation pictures, then your life will become hollow. You think posting pictures of your "luxury" life can make others jealous—only the mentally fragile will feel diminished from your pictures. Mentally healthy people can see right through your act. You think you get enhanced from showing off how great your life is; it is not you that gets inflated. It is your fictional self—made up of your digital and mental images—that gets inflated. Doing such things only makes you pettier—your soul is dying, and your phantom self is draining away from your life. Do you really want to live on behalf of a ghost?

Many people think that success means a fancy office building, high stock price, lots of funding, and lots of employees, so they end up putting all their energy and resources into pursuing such symbols. The symbols are only the consequence and not the cause of success. The symbols can only give people the appearance of being successful. Sooner or later, their symbols will fade if there's no intrinsic value in their work.

Paraphrasing a saying by Sadhguru: when one wants a flower, they don't even need to think flower, they just need to think of the soil, the manure, the seed, the water, and the sunlight—which doesn't resemble a flower at all—but if they take care of those things, then a flower will happen one day. Similarly with people wanting success; they don't need to think about what they will achieve, they only need to be dedicated to the process, and then depending on various factors, they will go as far as their dedication can take them. When people want the symbols more than the actual process, the symbols rarely materialize for them.

POLARIZATION

As the child's experience of the world gets pervaded with more and more conceptual knowledge, his mind will start to become more polarized. Because concepts can only exist in relationships, and the most predominant relationship would naturally gravitate toward the duality between himself and not himself (the world). To know himself, he needs to know the world and vice versa. Neither himself nor the world can exist alone in a conceptual reality. The two are needed for comparison; he can only know himself to be tall if he thinks that others are short; he can only know that he exists within a body if he thinks there is a world outside it; he can only know that there is a world if he thinks that he exists independent from it.

Once the mind gets its first split—between what is me and not me—then it will get endlessly fractured as it attempts to divide up every aspect of reality—like the thinker and the thought, the feeler and the feeling, the good and the bad, and so on. And the fragments of our mind will engage in endless friction—where one part of the mind wants to control the other—like the thinker over the thought.

> "And because we're split-minded, we're always dithering—Is the choice I'm about to make from the higher self or the lower self? Is it of the spirit or of the flesh? Is the message I received from God or the Devil? And nobody can decide, because if you knew how to choose, you wouldn't have to. You can think about it until you're blue, but you'll never get the answer, because the problems of life are so subtle that to try to solve them with vague principles—even if those vague principles come in the form of specific moral instructions—is completely impossible."[4] (Alan Watts, *Out of Your Mind*)

As the polarity—between the experiencer (me) and what is experienced (not me)—continues to develop within the child's psyche, he will experience himself more and more as an object—mental images—that is witnessed rather than the subject that is witnessing his experience. The child may first identify the experiencer (the me) to a sound, like the child's name or the word 'I,' which in the child's mind becomes a thought, and thus the initial 'I' thought is formed to represent the child. The child now thinks 'I' is who he is.

> "The next step are thoughts of me and mine to designate things that are somehow part of 'I.' ... When "my" toy breaks or is taken away, intense suffering arises. Not because of any in-

trinsic value that the toy has ... but because of the thought of 'mine.' The toy became part of the child's developing sense of self, of 'I.'"[5] (Eckhart Tolle)

The child's sense of self—the "me"—then absorbs more concepts to form a self-image. The initial self-image is typically composed of labels that he has gathered from his early interactions with other people. For example, his parents frequently referred to him by a name and made remarks on his characteristics. So, he starts to think of himself as an entity called John Doe and is male, Asian, tall, short, cute, ugly, polite, rude, and so on.

The labels like name, gender, race, physical attributes, and personality start off as just knowledge for the child. The child knows that he is male like he knows that the sky is blue. But as the child goes through experiences that involved discriminatory treatments towards him or others based on such labels. The labels start to take on different meanings for him as it gets further tangled up with his identity and emotions.

When the child witnesses social situations where good-looking people tend to receive a lot of attention, while the not-so-good looking ones tend to be ignored somewhat—and that combined with his own feelings toward people's appearances along with the experience of others treatment of him based on his appearance—he may start to judge people based on their appearance and make his appearance a large part of his identity. Subsequently, he may feel and act superior to others if he thinks he is good-looking, or feel inadequate and withdraw from social situations if he thinks that he is ugly.

When the child encounters discriminatory acts toward him based on his race, while also being exposed to anti-racist materials from school and media, he may start to see himself as a victim and develop feelings of acute anger and injustice around his race. So when he faces racist actions in the future, he may get extremely offended toward such behaviors, and resort to physical or verbal violence in retaliation rather than handling the situation in a calm manner. This pattern of thinking, feeling, and behaving on behalf of their identity as a separate entity forms the initial stages of the ego.

THE HIERARCHICAL GAME

As the child grows up, society will continue to condition his egoic qualities because most societies are rooted in the collective ego. The society wants the child to perpetuate their ego delusion by participating in their game of life—a game where you need to be a somebody in a hierarchical system—where individuals are compared on various metrics like appearance, wealth, possessions, accomplishments, capabilities, knowledge, popularity, etc. To get people to buy into this game, various reward systems are set-up by society to acknowledge people's progress like income, fame, power, recognition, and status.

The child's parents have already bought into the hierarchical game and have made their child's success part of their own ego. So they project their own fears and expectations onto the child by saying things like: "What do you want to be when you grow up? If you don't want to do menial jobs for the rest of your life, then you better study hard; if you don't want to end up alone for the rest of your life, then you better be more social and make more money; imagine how great your lifestyle can be if you become a CEO." When the child hears such things, it may not mean much to him at first. But when his parents start to compare him to other kids by saying stuff like: "your friend got better grades than you; your friend makes more money than you; your friend got a girlfriend before you did"—and then start to treat him based on such comparisons—the child learns to play a certain role to avoid punishment and reap the rewards like attention.

When the child develops more relationships in the world, he learns to play more roles as different people project different expectations onto him. He learned to get good grades, make lots of money, and act responsible and polite to impress his parents; he learned to be hard-working, efficient, and obedient to impress his boss and co-workers; he learned to perform well in sports, and act cool, funny and rebellious to impress his friends and romantic interests. As a result, the child learned to put on so many masks that he starts to forget his natural way of being.

When the child goes through puberty, his hormones will bring mate selection to the forefront of his mind. During this phase, comparisons of one to another in various attributes are further emphasized when it comes to being selected as a mate. And so, striving to be better than others may no longer be just a game to him, as he starts to take his roles seriously and really believe that he is a somebody in the world.

The child will begin to see people through the filter of his own hierarchy system. As a consequence, he will relate with others based on his own standing in the hierarchy, and then will project his own expectations back onto others—which perpetuates the collective ego game.

Typically during the child's high school years, the ego becomes predominant in his life. When this happens, the child's joy of simply existing will be veiled by the ego's need to achieve more. The child will start to impose conditions on his happiness because he thinks he should only be happy when certain criteria have been fulfilled. But even when fulfillment comes, he will not be able to enjoy it for long, as the ego will just quickly latch on to another milestone.

The more the child wants to progress faster than others in the hierarchical game, the more he will treat the present as only a means to an end. The child's experience of reality will be increasingly drawn to his mind—where everything is conceptualized—and the present has been divided into past and future. The child only sees himself as what he has been in the past and what he will be in the future. The child does not see himself as he actually is—which is always in the now. So the child lives in a state of perpetual division and contradiction. "The ego-self constantly pushes reality away. It constructs a future out of empty expectations and a past out of regretful memories."[6] (Deepak Chopra)

The future is not separate from the past. The future can only exist as the present, which is determined by the state of one's mind. And a mind that is conditioned by the past will recreate the same past—albeit in a different form. You were competing with people making 6 figures, and now you're competing with people making 7 figures; you have improved, but only superficially—your core is still competitive, still unsatisfied.

True satisfaction cannot come as long as the mind is stuck in time—where the mind has polarized the present into the past and future. A polarized mind is a conflicted mind, because the mind is always trying to escape from the past to arrive at a projected future. And a projected future can only be constructed from the past; you can only desire what you already know. You cannot desire something that was never in your experience. A projected future will always be an abstraction and thus will always conflict with the real future—which arrives as the present.

You feel inadequate, so you want to make 6 figures to feel adequate when compared to people making 5 figures. After you start making 6 figures, you still feel inadequate because there are people making 7 figures. The feeling of inadequacy is a fact. The ending of inadequacy with a high income is an idea. So the projected future never comes, and one's inner contradiction will develop into all sorts of psychological problems.

> "All negativity is caused by an accumulation of psychological time and denial of the present. Unease, anxiety, tension, stress, worry - all forms of fear - are caused by too much future, and not enough presence. Guilt, regret, resentment, grievances, sadness, bitterness, and all forms of nonforgiveness are caused by too much past, and not enough presence."[7]
> (Eckhart Tolle, *The Power of Now*)

The present moment cannot have problems. You cannot fear or resent the present, because the present is always whole and actual—you actually can do something if necessary. If no action is possible, you can accept the moment as it is. There's no internal conflict because it was outside of your control.

The past and the future are abstract—it gives you the illusion of control: "if I had only done that instead...; I can get there if I do this..." It breeds conflict between what is and what can be, which subsequently leads to fear and resentment. "I'm afraid of what may happen again; I'm afraid of not becoming what I want to be; I'm afraid of facing what I did; I'm angry about the way things went; I resent what they did to me."

When the child is trapped in time, the child is trapped in saṃsāra—the endless cycle of mundane existence and suffering. This is when two of the greatest faculties of being human—memory and imagination—start to become more of a detriment rather than an enhancement in one's life. (paraphrasing a saying by Sadhguru)

When the individual is suffering, the ego tries to alleviate the unpleasant feelings by the only way it knows how—which is to fix some external situation. It typically involves achieving some future goal—which implies time. Of course, some temporary pleasure can be gained from that, however, very soon the suffering returns because the ego is never satisfied with the present moment. So again, the ego tries to do more, to arrive, to become.

The ego is always centered on doing rather than being; this is why most societies—especially the capitalistic ones—tend to value the youth and neglect the elderly because they can only see the value in doing, in achieving. Capitalistic societies prioritize profit over everything else. As Milton Friedman wrote: "there is one and only one social responsibility of business – to use its resources and engage in activities designed to increase its profits."[8]

Most people have invested so much of their identity in the hierarchical game that they are completely lost in it. People have invested in clothes, skincare, fitness, and plastic surgery to develop a certain look; undergone rigorous schooling to get their qualifications; sacrificed their time and energy to reach a certain spot on the corporate ladder, and have accumulated various possessions to establish their status in life.

People remain stuck in the rat race because they always believe that the next milestone is just around the corner—so they can finally surpass their competitors. Stopping now would risk being surpassed by others and losing what they have accumulated —which to the ego would feel like death.

The ego does not see any other alternative in living life, because it has a tendency to attract circumstances and other egos to reinforce its own mental perspective. The ego is always comparing themselves to people who are more accomplished than them. From the perspective of those that they look up to, the result of their suffering is that they aren't successful enough—so they should strive harder. This cycle of striving continues until the ego generates so much suffering and exhaustion that a greater intelligence of the body steps in to force a shut down of the ego activity—either psychologically in the form of a nervous break-down or physically in the form of various illnesses.

When the ego shuts down, some people may get snapped out of their delusions and awaken to the reality out of their mind—the present moment. Such experiences are sometimes described by people to be mystical, as the experience may be accompanied by a state of deep peace and ecstasy —which to some people is a sharp contrast to their typical distressed state.

In Zen, such an experience is called a satori—which means a momentary glimpse into your true nature as awareness, as the present moment. The glimpse is only momentary because the mind cannot grasp the experience conceptually. The present moment is as it is; there's nothing to grasp. So the mind falls back into its familiar thinking framework—where reality is conceptualized. Where the mind can continue playing its delusional hierarchical game—striving to achieve more, accumulate more.

> "Ego-identification with things creates attachment to things, obsession with things, which in turn creates our consumer society and economic structures where the only measure of progress is always *more*. The unchecked striving for more, for endless growth, is a dysfunction and a disease. It is the same dysfunction the cancerous cell manifests, whose only goal

is to multiply itself, unaware that it is bringing about its own destruction by destroying the organism of which it is a part."[9] (Eckhart Tolle, *A New Earth*)

WHO ARE YOU?

The ego's core is a misidentification, so its exterior is always shaky. That's why we hear people saying things like: "I'm trying to find myself, I'm so lost, I don't know who I am anymore." How could one not know themselves? Shouldn't the understanding of one's own self be one's most fundamental understanding? However, this is not the case for most people.

Today, we have knowledge about so many things, from space travel to quantum physics to A.I., but we don't know the slightest thing about the nature of ourselves. This is because we have attempted to know ourselves through the accumulation of mental concepts, which builds up to a self-image.

Mental concepts can never be stable, and so our self-image undergoes continuous change. When we were 12 years old, we think we are like this, and then when we were 20 years old, we think we are like that, and this goes on throughout our lives. We always think that our current self-image is the most accurate one, but end up wrong every time when we look back at ourselves a few years later and see how silly we used to be.

Most people believe that there is something within us that makes you "you," and this characteristic is unique to you, never change, and will continue on forever. If you believe in a heaven or life after death, what form would you appear in your afterlife? If it resembles your physical form, at which biological age would your afterlife form resemble? Isn't life always in a state of continuous change? And if our afterlife form does resemble our physical form, then why does our physical form disintegrate at all? Do you think that the Creator would recreate the exact same thing again somewhere else after transforming the original?

And why are we so attached to our forms? Is it because we cannot face the fact that our physical and psychological form will come to an end? Do we not see that every living thing has to relinquish its body upon death? Whatever that has a beginning will have an end, as all forms are ephemeral. If we cannot bring our forms with us, then why the belief in a heaven? What good are carnal and mental pleasures without a form? "You came empty handed, and you will leave empty handed." (*Bhagavad Gita*)

Throughout our lives, we have been deeply ingrained with the belief that the "me" is a character with fixed traits, especially from the various kinds of media that we have consumed since childhood

—like books, movies, shows, and video games. We always see that the characters are portrayed with a fixed personality, motive, and capability—and character developments occur in a believable manner. If the characters' motives do not come from believable sources, or if the characters deviate from their expected reactions and behaviors, then we call it bad writing or unrealistic. This book is not justifying bad writing in literature; this book is pointing to the influence of literature on our beliefs.

We see that people in the real world are also treated (to an extent) as a character with fixed traits. When public figures make major decisions in their life (like career moves, lifestyle choices, or new ideologies), they typically have to provide some justifiable reasons for their actions. If their justifications don't align with our conception of who they were in the past, then we make up their hidden motives according to how we understand them (and sometimes we get it right, relatively speaking). If the public figure's actions significantly deviate from what we think they should do, then we say things like: "he's lost his mind; he got brainwashed; he lost his way; he's no longer himself."

When a star athlete gives an off-performance in a crucial game, we hear sports commentators (like Stephen A. Smith for example) say things like: "I don't know who was playing that game; he did not show up; some impersonator must've showed up in his place; somebody must've drugged him." The public always constructs a narrative surrounding an athlete's performance—the importance of the game, the rivalry between the teams, and the circumstances leading up to the game—so that we can feel like we know what kind of player they are, based on their performances.

If a star athlete repeatedly deviates from the kind of performances that we expect from him, then we develop our own narratives about the athlete: "he's going through personal issues; his heart is not in the game anymore; he's no longer the player he used to be." If a star athlete only under-performs in crucial games, then we call him names like: "not clutch", a "choker."

The statements that we make about other people may be true relative to certain contexts. However, this book is not concerned with the "truthfulness" of our statements. Rather, this book is pointing to our tendency to project images and narratives about other people and then take those images to be the truth. Because then, we do not see people—including ourselves—as they are. Instead, we can only see images—which is always a distortion of reality.

The fictional world rarely treats all the characters equally. The fictional world always treats the characters hierarchically to illustrate their intended value—which always resides in some form of quality like their appearance, personality, capability, or achievements. This happens in the real world as well—we see that celebrities like actors, artists, and athletes are judged on a similar set of criteria on media outlets. The ones who compare favourably in those criteria get showered with attention and praises, while those lacking in those criteria get neglected and made fun of. Such discriminative social dynamics reinforce the belief that all a human being is—and worth—is their qualities. So we become increasingly identified with our qualities.

We are not caricatures; our beliefs, capabilities, and personalities can change at random without good explainable reason. This is why we have so much problems in our relationships. We treat other people as if they are going to remain the same person throughout their entire life. We get mad at them when they break their word, but how can anybody keep their word? Their word is made by their past self who had an entirely different situation, ideology, and emotional state —which is almost like an entirely different person —and hence marriages fail approximately 50% of the time.

To most of us, the "me" is like an idea, a story, that exists only within our memory; without memory, the "me" disappears. If you believe in reincarnation and are trying to live a virtuous life so that your next life can be better—what is it that will carry over? Without memory—you would be a completely different person, just like how you don't feel like you were ever reincarnated into your current life now, because you have no recollection of who you were in your past lives.

If you strongly identify yourself as your biology and believe that the "you" is being carried over via genetic information, then after you die and wake up in another body with different genes, how would you treat your previous genetic line? (of course you wouldn't know, but let's say you do) Would you treat them as other than you? As a competitor?

Similarly, if you strongly identify yourself as an idea, and believe that the "you" is being carried over via the opinions of other people, then after you die and wake up in another body, how would you treat your previous character? (again, assuming you know) Suppose you were regarded as the "greatest basketball player of all time" in your previous life and are a basketball player again in this life. Would you treat your previous character as someone to surpass? As a hindrance to you becoming the greatest in this life? And feel like you have to live in its shadow? Do you see the absurdity in identifying yourself as anything at all? What if you are in every single sentient being simultaneously—how would you treat other beings? Would you harbour hatred, jealousy, and envy towards them?

Even memory is ultimately unreliable, you may have faint memories of being different people or creatures in your dreams, but when you wake up, their reality is entirely gone as if they've never existed. Even the memories of your own past feel kind of like a dream. When you look back at yourself in photos, videos taken 10, 20 years old—you can't fathom ever being that person, because that reality is entirely gone and will never happen again—there's a kind of unrealness to them.

What continues from form to form is formless, unchanging, and everlasting; it has no objective qualities. It is *that* which knows your experience, the pure witness, the Soul, Awareness, God. However, if you don't experientially know it as a fact, then you can only believe in it or don't, but neither can bring you closer to the truth. One direct way of knowing it is simply asking yourself: what is it that is aware of my experience? And the answer is either there or it isn't. You cannot invent an answer through thought, because if you do, then it will be just another belief, another theory, which can be challenged, changed, and taken away from you. To hold on to your beliefs, you need to constantly protect them, so inevitably, it will turn into your belief vs. my belief and your God vs. my God, which is the cause of all the conflict we see in religions. "The Tao that can be told is not the eternal Tao"[10] (Lao Tzu)

Most people think that consciousness is personal —meaning that it carries their personal identity with its memories, beliefs, and so on. So if they can upload their consciousness to a new body, then they can experience the world through the lens of their identity in that body. People are equating their identity to consciousness. The identity is memory—which is form; it is the content of consciousness but not consciousness itself. Consciousness is the formless, the unmanifested —which is the source for all manifestations, all phenomena. People are mistaking the form for the formless, the consequence for the source, the movie for the screen. The ability to experience and the ability to experience from a certain memory are two different things; if you had amnesia or dementia, then the "you" with all your memories would disappear, but you can still experience. So are you memory? Or are you consciousness?

> "We learn, very thoroughly ... to identify ourselves with an equally conventional view of 'myself.' For the conventional 'self' or 'person' is composed mainly of a history consisting of selected memories... According to convention, I am not simply what I am doing now. I am also what I have done, and my conventionally edited version of my past is made to seem almost more the real 'me' than what I am at this moment. For what I am seems so fleeting and intangible, but what I was is fixed and final.

It is the firm basis for predictions of what I will be in the future, and so it comes about that I am more closely identified with what no longer exists than with what actually is!"[11] (Alan Watts, *The Way of Zen*)

Because people have mistaken their memory for consciousness, then they subsequently think that they can somehow separate their mind from their body. Our mind, with its memories and beliefs, is the composition of the physical elements in the body. The chemical processes in the body are reflected as the psychological processes in the mind; you cannot separate the two. If the physical composition changes—brain injury for example—then the psychological composition will also change—like loss of memory, and change of personality.

There was a book called *A Change of Heart* where Claire Sylvia wrote about her experiences after undergoing a heart and lung transplant. Her personality and cravings started to change after the transplant. When she later discovered who her donor was—she found out that her newly developed cravings and personality were very similar to the cravings and personality that her donor had. The body and the mind are intrinsically connected; all physical forms carry an energy frequency that is reflected in the psychological form, and all forms are the vibrations of the same formless energy—Consciousness.

CHAPTER THREE:
THE EGO'S MASK

WHAT ARE YOU?

What we conceive as a person is nothing but a temporary pattern of physical and psychological composition. Your body is essentially just an accumulation of food. Your mind, which consists of your memories, beliefs, attachments, dreams, and personality, is just an accumulation of impressions. Even your inclinations, karmic imprints, astrological influences, and genetic instructions are derived from energy patterns of the universe. What exactly can you point to to claim your independent existence?

We believe that we are a foreign agent that came into the universe—and thus has to conquer nature as if it is something fundamentally different from us, something external, chaotic, and hostile. In truth, not only did we came out of the universe and will go back into it, but we are also made out of it. We are not some independent thing that is doing something to the universe; we are what the universe is *doing*. We think we are a body, a static thing, but our body is an activity, a process in which constant transactions are going on between our internal organs and the external environment (the respiration process for example), but we are never a constant.

> "Just as the flame of a candle is never a constant. A flame of a candle is a stream of hot gas. Only, you say 'the flame of the candle' as if it were a constant. Well, it is a recognizably constant pattern: the spear-shaped outline of the flame and its coloration is a constant pattern. But in exactly the same way, we are all constant patterns, and that's all we are; the only thing constant about us at all is the doing rather than the being. It's the way we behave, the way we dance; only there's no 'we' that dances, there's just the dancing."[1] (Alan Watts)

There was an old philosophical paradox called the Ship of Theseus, where Plutarch questions that if a ship were to entirely replaced—piece by piece—then would the ship still be the same ship? This question could be applied to us also; all of our cells will get replaced multiple times during our lifespan, so are we still the same person? If we approach the problem with our conceptual mind, where our thoughts have cut up reality into fragments, then we will be caught in a contradiction, and thereby the problem remains a paradox. This is because we are trying to solve the problem while first assuming the false to be true. "We cannot solve our problems with the same level of thinking that created them." (Albert Einstein)

When we think that there are static "things" in the universe, then we are imposing our mental concepts on existence. In actuality, there was never a "thing" that is a ship; a ship is a process in which it is changing every second, albeit very minimally, but nevertheless, it is changing. Of course, we do need to refer to it as a "thing" in our daily lives for communication purposes, but we must not be trapped by our language and recognize that language is ultimately a representation of reality but not reality itself.

If we see that everything in existence is a process, then Plutarch's problem would no longer be a paradox, and subsequently its question would collapse. We can also see the various misconceptions that we have held about ourselves, we believe that we are an organism with a particular body and mind, and so if there is an exact replica of that, then our clone would be the same person as us. There can never be an exact person, because our clones can never have the same perception, thought, and sensations as us, as their experience will deviate from us as soon as they come into existence. Thus, they will accumulate a different memory. We are actually not the same person moment to moment either, because our memory and cells are constantly changing.

If we see that everything in existence is just a temporary pattern, then we can also recognize that everything is interconnected, because they are all changing into one another all the time; what was one thing now becomes another. The universe is an inseparable whole, in which nothing can exist in isolation—including ourselves. If the universe does not exist as it is (gravity, atmospheric composition, the sun, etc.), then we can't exist as we are.

> "Your existence is not something that is just the hopeless little creature that's suddenly confronted with a great big external world that ... eats him up. Every tiniest little thing that comes into being ... I will go so far as to say is an event upon which this whole cosmos depends. Because this thing goes both ways: it's not only that every little organism which exists depends on its total environment. The reverse is also true: that the total environment depends on each and every one of those little organisms."[1] (Alan Watts)

For most of us, we have become so hypnotized by our conceptual mind that we never see the unity of all things. Our fragmented perception of reality and have identified ourselves as an independent existence separated by our skins, and we have been thinking, feeling, and acting on behalf of this phantom entity—that is, the ego.

THE PHANTOM IDENTITY

The ego ends up assuming your identity and will pretend to live your life as if it were real. In actuality, it's just an illusion and inherently unstable. So the ego is continuously seeking security—and it does so by constantly labeling itself with concepts thinking that it can bring aggrandizement and solidity to itself.

Examples of concepts that we define ourselves with include Christian, Democrat, Capitalist, Caucasian, Scorpio, mother, athlete, engineer, successful, cool, attractive, rich, poor, smart, dumb, and so on. All such definitions are ultimately concocted within our minds, so they will always be an abstraction and can never substitute the real thing. Our misidentification of ourselves can become so abstract that we can see people saying things like: "I am the G.O.A.T. (short for greatest of all time); I am the king; I am an icon; I am justice; I am vengeance; I am legend; I am God."

"The state of presence – the sense 'I am' or 'I

exist' – is natural for everyone. No one needed to teach you this. When this sense 'I am' combines itself or becomes associated with other states and ideas, it is as if those states become a part of what 'I am' is. But they are not original to who we are.

... The concept *I am the body* is the core belief we adopt very early on. Once we have accepted this basic *I am the body* concept as who we are, other concepts can now pour on top of it: I am a man or a woman...I am like this or that. And so a unique psychological identity forms.

Mostly we assume that this identity is an unquestionable fact, and yet those acquired beliefs are not part of our original nature. We take ourselves to be a particular body with a unique personality, and this perspective remains with us as we live our lives."[2] (Mooji, *Vaster Than Sky, Greater Than Space*)

When we identify ourselves as anything in the world—we are limiting ourselves, because we are trying to enclose that which is formless and limitless. No matter what we identify ourselves with, it will always be biased and thus limited. So if we try to navigate through life with our identity, then we will miss the infinite possibilities beyond our limited selves.

Suppose I strongly identify myself as an anti-social person because I had awful social experiences in the past. But if I maintain an open mind and continue to attempt new social events, maybe I could find some to be enjoyable and subsequently develop my social skills, which will dismantle my anti-social identity and liberate me from my limiting beliefs. But if I continue to avoid social interactions due to who I think I was in the past, then in that case I will never find out, and hence I will severely limit my possibilities for the rest of my life.

Suppose I strongly identify myself as an expert in a particular field, because I have more experience and more accomplishments than anybody else in that field. And if a beginner approached me with a possible solution to a problem that I wasn't able to solve for a long time—I may dismiss their suggestion and say something on the lines of: "it will never work, I've been at this problem for 10 years and if I can't solve it by now, then it is not solvable." So consequently, I may miss other possibilities due to my identity's biased perspective. "In the beginner's mind there are many possibilities, but in the expert's there are few."[3] (Shunryu Suzuki)

> "Once your intellect … gets identified with something, you function within the realm of this identity. Whatever you are identified with, all your thoughts and emotions spring from that identity. … Whatever your thoughts and emotions, these identifications are a certain level of prejudice. In fact, your mind is itself a certain kind of prejudice. Why? Because

it functions from limited data and is fronted by an essentially discriminatory intellect. So, your mind, which should have been a ladder to the divine, is stumbling through endless mediocrity and, on some occasions, has become a straight stairway to hell."[4] (Sadhguru, *Inner Engineering*)

The longer we abide by our identities, the more real our identities are to us, and eventually, they will become us. When most people say or think: "I this..., I that..., or I believe...," it's not even them that are doing it, but actually, their identity is doing it in their place. And for many of us, our identities are not even consciously built by us—we just inherited them from our environment, so we live our entire lives on other people's behalf. We are pursuing success based on other people's definitions of success. We are conducting ourselves based on other people's expectations.

When we were young, we had all kinds of dreams, all kinds of ideas on what we wanted to do—we didn't want to be like the adults who only cared about money, their image, and other superficial things. But when we grew up, we become conditioned by our society—we ended up just like those adults; we talk like them, think like them, and behave like them. We made other people's goals our goals. We invested all our energy into pursuing the same superficial things that those adults cared about. We got married, got a secure job, and lived the rest of our days for our vacations and pensions. All the possibilities we dreamt up as a kid are now gone. Our phantom identity now dictates our life; we have become a slave to our identity.

> "Imagine what would happen instead if you were able to take your attention off the physical world and the environment. ... When you take your attention off your body, you become no body ... When you take your attention off the people in your life, you become no one—and so you no longer have an identity as a parent, a partner ... You have no race, no gender ... When you take your attention off objects and places in the physical environment, you are in no thing and no where. Finally, if you take your attention off linear time ... you are in no time—you are in the present moment, in which all possibilities in the quantum field exist. Because you are no longer identifying with or connected to the physical world, you are no longer trying to affect matter with matter—you are beyond matter and beyond how you [identify] yourself as a body in space and time ...

> The moment that happens, you unfold your attention and energy into an unknown field beyond matter where all possibilities exist—a field made up of nothing but invisible frequencies carrying information or consciousness. And just like the quantum scientists who

took their attention off the electron only to find that it reverted to energy and possibility, if you were to take your attention off your life or get beyond the memory of your life, your life should turn into possibility. After all, if you focus on the known, you get the known. If you focus on the unknown, you create a possibility. The longer you can linger in that field of infinite possibilities as an awareness ... the more you are going to create a new experience or new possibilities in your life."[5] (Joe Dispenza, *Becoming Supernatural*)

We think that once we have an identity—like a CEO, a champion, a husband—then we have security, because: we have become a somebody; we belong somewhere; we have someone to love us; we have people that respect us—but is this really security? Our loved one could leave us; we could lose our job and reputation. So we need to struggle to maintain our identity constantly, and we are always afraid of the unknown, which can destroy our identity—is this really security? We need to seek physical security such as food and shelter for survival purposes, but why do we seek psychological security?

"Because we want to be inwardly secure, we are constantly seeking methods and means for this security, and thereby we create authority, the worship of another, which destroys comprehension, that spontaneous tranquility of

> mind in which alone there can be a state of creativeness."[6] (Jiddu Krishnamurti)

Therefore, the more psychologically secure we become, the duller we become, which makes us more demanding for security and so more prone to disturbances. If we have everyone praising us, then the minute they don't—our entire world collapses; the harder we build up our false self, the harder we will fall. So when we inflate ourselves with others' praises, we are also making ourselves more dependent on others' opinions of us and so more prone to others' insults. This is why, even though physical security has never been an issue for most of us, and yet, we constantly feel insecure. So we try to cling to some definition of ourselves, thinking it can give us security.

All definitions are separative; I can only define myself as successful if I define others as failures; I can only define myself as a believer of God if I define others as non-believers; I can only define myself as enlightened if I define others as non-enlightened. With every definition, I am further separating myself from humanity. For every group that I try to belong to, simultaneously, I am also excluding myself from many more groups. While I am constructing my own identity, I am also constructing the other, the enemy: "I am not those kinds of people; do not associate me with those losers; I am right, they're wrong; I don't want to go there, people there may not like me because of what I represent."

As the ego accumulates more and more definitions onto itself, it becomes increasingly alienated in the world—is this really security? "To put it still more plainly: the desire for security and the feeling of insecurity are the same thing. To hold your breath is to lose your breath."[7] (Alan Watts)

The ego will eventually cover itself with so many definitions there isn't a person on earth that can match up to all of it. When the ego is facing some antagonism with every person that it encounters —the ego will conjure up a person that will save it from its alienation; an imaginary person that can finally understand and accept all of the ego's iden- tities—which the ego calls: the "one," the "soul- mate."

The beauty and fun of life are in its diversity and not in its homogeneity—can you stand an- other person that is exactly the same as you? The strength of a relationship is the ability of each partner to complement the other. If both part- ners have identical perspectives, they are more likely to be stuck in the same life patterns; they will strengthen each other's delusions rather than shattering them. Also, can two minds that are so antagonistic really form a genuine relationship? When they are not busy putting up walls between themselves, they will just put up walls between themselves and everyone else. They will go from a "me vs the world" to an "us vs the world," so they have managed to reduce some alienation, but not by much.

When people feel alienated from their surroundings, they will naturally need confidence in navigating through the world. This is why many people focus on improving their self-esteem, self-confidence, and self-worth. The problem with their approach is that their confidence is centered on a "self." Hence, they need a reason to feel good about themselves. Such a reason always has to come externally—from comparison with others.

So people's confidence fluctuates between superiority and inferiority depending on the external situation. If they are partaking in an activity where they are considered better than everyone else, then they would feel superior. However, if they are in an environment where their traits aren't valued as much, then they feel inferior.

True worthiness cannot be derived externally—it cannot come from any comparison. Once the "self" that needs to feel good about itself, that needs to feel deserving of love—ceases to be—then true worthiness emerges from within the depths of one's very being as the formless, as Awareness, as God. True worthiness is not centered on a "self;" it is not comparative, as in more superior than so and so. Therefore it doesn't have an opposite; it's not worthiness as opposed to unworthiness; it's beyond the concept of worthiness and unworthiness. It is there as a fact, so it's not threatened by any external circumstance.

Typically when people try to improve their self-confidence, they either try to convince themselves why they are better than others in certain areas, or they try to improve some aspect of themselves —like their appearance, their wealth, the importance of their job, the number of friends that they have, and so on. However, people's qualities will be nonexistent if no one acknowledges them, so they need to constantly seek validation from others to keep their self-image intact; when others acknowledge how good they look, how popular they are, and how successful they are, then they feel good about themselves.

PHANTOM RELATIONSHIPS

When people interact with others on behalf of their self-image, then the interaction becomes a transaction, and thereby inauthentic. The agenda of the interaction is no longer to relate to the other, but rather to extract something from the other—acknowledgement, attention, or physical intimacy—so that their own image can be enhanced. "Look at the partner I'm with; look at how many people I know; look at what these people are saying about me." Thus, the human beings are not interacting; and instead, it's the images that are interacting.

I have an image of who I am, and I'm relating to you based on the image I have of you. If I have an image of myself as an important person and you as a trivial person, then I may talk down to you and expect you to respect me. And if I have an image of you as a more accomplished person than me, then I may look up to you and try to impress you. So I'm not relating to you as you are, and instead, I'm relating to you as an image that I have constructed of you. And you may be relating to me as an image you have constructed of me. We are constantly strengthening these images from the opinions that we gather from our interactions, so it's the images that are in a relationship. Hence our relationships are always full of conflict; conflict between the images and conflict between the image and the human being.

We need to play a role to satisfy not only others' images of us but also our own images of ourselves. We also need others to play their role so that our images of others and ourselves don't get disturbed. All this role-playing requires a tremendous amount of energy, so for close relationships —where we spend a lot of time with our partner— our energy will be drained sooner or later. When our masks come off, our relationship will crumble since it was never our authentic selves that were in a relationship in the first place.

When our masks come off, the problematic side of our egos will show itself—that's when we start to get needy, manipulative, and antagonistic: "if you don't behave the way I expect you to; if you don't make me feel like who I think I am; if you don't respect me; if you don't satisfy my desires, then I have a problem with you; then I will take away my love from you; then I will destroy you." There is no humanity, no love in these kinds of relationships. How can we claim that we love the other person when we merely see them as a means for our own gains? Does real love turn into hate when our beloved no longer behaves in accordance with our expectations? Is love a form of control?

True love is unconditional. It gives the freedom for people to be as they are. Most people think that unconditional love simply means willing to be with someone no matter what—this is especially easy to do for people who are already easy to get along with or people you have to be with for the rest of your life anyway. People say, "I unconditionally love my parents and my dog," but that's not unconditional love: they love them on the condition that they are your parents or your dog.

True love cannot discriminate in any form, so love cannot be something you do, because any doing will always be rooted in duality—a lover and a beloved. Such a love will always be discriminatory; "I love you and not them." When love is rooted in duality, then it becomes rooted in selfishness and will just turn into a form of possessiveness. The emotional aspect of that love will contain its own polar opposites like hate, jealousy, and fear; you love your partner, but you also fear your partner leaving. If your partner flirts with someone else, then your love will instantly flip to hate and jealousy. Therefore, true love must be the way you are and not what you do. If you look at a puppy, the puppy is one with life and so they are love; you can feel their love without them saying a thing.

"Love is not selective, desire is selective. In love there are no strangers. When the centre of selfishness is no longer, all desires for pleasure and fear of pain cease; one is no longer interested in being happy; beyond happiness there is pure intensity, inexhaustible energy, the ecstasy of giving from a perennial source."[8] (Nisargadatta Maharaj)

For most of us, love has become just a phrase, a lie that we use to make things go our way. We say "I love you" to others, so they can stay by our side, so they can sleep with us. In other words, we don't love; we just want others to give us security and sexual gratification. When love is turned into an idea, then it becomes tainted and corrupted. An idea is always rooted in memory—which is in the past—and therefore dead. True love is alive. It is always in the present, always new, and thus has no past.

"Love is love, not to be defined or described by the mind as exclusive or inclusive. Love is its own eternity: it is the real, the supreme, the immeasurable."[9] (Aldous Huxley)

As long as our past identity is there, there can be no love. If we are completely aware of this, then our identity will start to dissolve. But we are not aware because our identity is always in control and takes up so much of our attention. And since our identity's existence is dependent on mental concepts—it needs to be continuously sustained by the mind in the form of thought patterns to persist itself. This is why most people think incessantly. Their thoughts are constantly constructing a dream world to veil reality as it is, so that this dream world can uphold the idea of who they think they are.

Most people have become so absorbed in their psychological processes that they are rarely aware of it when it goes on—this is like an A.I. program functioning through its programming without being able to look at and modify its own code. When a person becomes inseparable from their thoughts, they start to believe that they are their thoughts, as illustrated by René Descartes' famous statement: "I think, therefore I am." The thought patterns end up operating continuously in their mind like background processes in a computer; they are kind of like parasites living off of an individual's psychic energy.

Each thought pattern is like a voice in the head revolving around an imaginary entity. The entities are supported by various belief structures and emotionally charged memories. Each entity emanates an energy field that vibrates at a certain frequency. This energy field tunes into—and subsequently attracts—surrounding situations and people with a similar frequency. Such situations and people are more likely to provoke the entity's stored emotional charges, which in turn cause the entity's identity to be reenacted. This is why we can see some people tend to get into the same life scenarios over and over again.

An ego with strong self-victimizing beliefs tend to get into relationships with abusive partners; an ego with heavy anger charges tend to get into fights and shouting matches with other angry egos; an ego with a strong fear of making a fool of itself in social situations tend to get into embarrassing situations often, so they end up avoiding them as much as they can. You may find such people complain to you about their life situations all the time—telling you how much they hate them. But their ego wants them because their situations not only reinvigorate their phantom identity, but also validates why their beliefs were right, even though it was their beliefs that created their situations in the first place. So people end up trapped in not only a dream world within their mind but also a dream-like world in their external reality—where they continuously suffer the same situations.

THE CONFLICTED MIND

If all of the ego's mental entities were to be unveiled, you would find that the central figure—the "you"—that the entities are revolving around (and are supposed to represent) is not actually there. The ego does not want that to be discovered because it fears being a nobody, so it always cloaks itself with a myriad of entities. Each entity has its own distinct identity and wants to grow and dominate, so they end up in conflict with one another all the time. The ego always lives in a fragmented existence and constantly wastes energy through its internal friction.

Our racial identity conflict with our national identity; our identity as someone who can sleep with many people conflict with our identity as a loyal partner; our identity as someone who doesn't care about what others think conflict with our identity as a likeable person; our role as a consumer conflict with our role as an employee in a consumer exploitative company; our desire to pursue our dreams conflict with our desire to remain in a secure job and relationship; our desire to be someone who is more successful than their friend/partner conflict with our desire to be someone who genuinely want their friend/partner to be successful; our desire to be what others want us to be conflict with our desire to be we want to be; our familial obligations conflict with our lovers obligations; our investor obligations conflict with our customer obligations; our client obligations conflict with our employer obligations; our behavior amongst our friends conflict with our behavior amongst our co-workers, our religious teachings conflict with our company's principles; our belief formed from a lesson learned in the past conflict with what we think we should do now. To live with all these contradictions within ourselves, we have become indecisive, corrupted, and hypocritical.

The conflict between opposing forces in existence is inevitable, as they are what keeps the game of existence going. No polarity in existence can completely destroy its opposite, as the destruction of its opposite would bring its own destruction also. If all death were to be eradicated, then to be alive would lose all its meaning. If all chaos were to go, then order would go as well. If human beings were somehow able to eliminate all the viruses, then the ecosystem that sustains human life would be disrupted, and subsequently all human life would end.

In the composition of the universe, there is conflict on every order of life, like viruses vs. immunity cells, and predators vs. preys. The conflicts between different organisms are what sustain the complex systems of life—from an ecosystem to a human being. So from another perspective, the different organisms are not really in conflict, but rather, they are in cooperation to keep nature in balance. Therefore, outward conflict and conflict between forms are sometimes necessary, but for us—psychologically and inwardly—why is there conflict?

As long as we don't know the actuality of what is, that is, the nature of the universe, of ourselves, and of existence itself—there will inevitably be conflict. There can only be one truth, but the number of falsities can be infinite. Whatever we don't know ourselves, we will form a belief about it from something that somebody else has said, and then we think we know.

We listen to religious leaders, professors, self-help teachers, entrepreneurs, and family members, and they all say different things. Some say reality is like this while others say it's like that; some say we should do this while others say we should do that. If we listen to one individual long enough, they will start to contradict themself. Even the things that we had learned from our own experiences are sometimes contradictory; what used to work no longer works anymore. So we are not really sure about anything; we don't know how life works, and we don't know how we ourselves work. We think doing one thing will lead to one result, but something else happens. So consequently, we are suffering from everything in life; we suffer when we get what we want, and we suffer when we don't get what we want. We suffer from our employment and marriage, and we suffer from being unemployed and single.

The more beliefs that we accumulate in our heads, the more confused we become. Yet, we don't discard our beliefs; instead, we try to patch up our confusion with even more beliefs. We don't realize that our beliefs have no effect on reality; reality will always be reality, it can never be threatened by falsities.

> "You are never dedicated to something you have complete confidence in. No one is fanatically shouting that the sun is going to rise tomorrow. They know it's going to rise tomorrow. When people are fanatically dedicated to political or religious faiths or any other kinds of dogmas or goals, it's always because these dogmas or goals are in doubt."[10] (Robert M. Pirsig)

What is true needs no belief; you do not need to believe in the earth to be round for it to be round. It is already round whether you believe in it or not.

So isn't it important for us to know something for ourselves? Rather than forming beliefs about it? We don't know whether there is a God or not, so we read some religious texts, and they say there is a God, or we read some scientist's conclusion, and they say there is no God. And once we have accepted others' words to be true, our curiosity and longing to know stops, and we stop paying attention to the nature of existence and of ourselves. If we always adopt what others have said, then we become—as Jiddu Krishnamurti called it—"second-hand people."

Why can't we admit that we don't know and be okay with that? Is it because we are afraid to face our own stupidity and inadequacy? We can't face ourselves, so we escape to a belief, a philosophy. Then we try to go through life with our heads full of distorted concepts and then taking them to be reality—thinking that we know what we are doing. Invariably, we will make all kinds of mistakes and cause all sorts of problems in life.

The most fundamental mistake that we have made is identifying ourselves as a separate fragment either in the mind or the world. Because once there is a separation between the experiencer and the experienced, there will inevitably be conflict, as the experiencer will want to control what is experienced—thoughts, feelings, and situations—not realizing that to control is to be controlled.

A mind that is one with experience lets things be as they are, and so does not need to control, and is free of conflict, of contradiction. Only the mind that desires things to go a certain way needs to control, and so it's being controlled—by its own desires. When I try to control myself and external events, I have projected an image of what I should be and how things should go, and my images, my expectations, now dictate my actions.

> "We are so well trained that we are our own domesticator. We are an autodomesticated animal. We can now domesticate ourselves according to the same belief system we were given, and using the same system of punishment and reward. We punish ourselves when we don't follow the rules according to our belief system; we reward ourselves when we are the 'good boy' or 'good girl'."[11] (Miguel Ruiz, *The Four Agreements*)

The more that I desire my projections to come true, the more that I'm restrained by them. So I —the controller—is being controlled by the ideals that I—the controller—has projected. Therefore, the controller is the controlled, and our inner contradiction will result in endless outer conflict, because the inner and the outer is one also.

The world is a reflection of ourselves; what we are inwardly, we will create outwardly; competitive people will be surrounded by competition; harmonious people will be surrounded by harmony. Society is not apart from the individual, it is created from the network of relationships that are formed between the individuals, and the kind of relationships formed are determined by each individual's inner state. Divisive individuals will create a divided society; whole individuals will create a unified society.

The world is also our body, the processes of thinking, respiration, and digestion are not isolated within our skins. The society provides our minds with impressions, the trees provide our lungs with oxygen, the ecosystem provides our stomachs with food, and the atmospheric process provides our bodies with fresh water. "There is no outer and inner process; there is only one unitary process, it is a whole, total movement, the inner movement expressing itself as the outer and the outer reacting again on the inner."[12] (Jiddu Krishnamurti)

Karma does not mean that the consequences from our actions may one day come back to get us, although the universe has those kinds of forces also. What karma really means is that any action we do onto others, we are also doing that very act to ourselves instantly. When we harm others, we are also generating a tremendous amount of negativity within ourselves, because we can only badly mistreat others as if we deeply feel unworthy of ourselves. Our inner negative energy will work itself out over the course of our life, which gets us into various detrimental circumstances. As the Buddha said: "Holding on to anger is like grasping a hot coal with the intent of throwing it at someone else; you are the one who gets burned."

Our harmful acts will also induce negative energy in others, and unless the victim is conscious enough to allow the negativity to flow through them, they will be psychologically wounded. Their own trapped negativity will ripple outwardly, affecting the surrounding world. Therefore, when we are being divisive, we are polluting not only our inner body, but we are also polluting our outer body that is the world.

We will continue to be divisive as long as we identify ourselves as a separate fragment, as an ego, because then it's me vs. you, and my agenda vs. your agenda; I always need to conquer you. So we remain trapped in the karmic cycle of death and rebirth—where one is continually reborn as a separate self in conflict with the other, and as a result suffering continues.

Our individual egos have conglomerated into collective egos. Our collective divisiveness has created a divided world, a world in constant conflict between nations, generations, races, genders, ideologies, sports teams, and religions. We have the US vs. China, Black vs. White, men vs. women, Socialism vs. Capitalism, Left vs. Right politics, baby boomers vs. millennials, Lakers vs. Celtics, and

Christianity vs. Islam. The ego wants the conflicts, the wars, because it gets strengthened when it's united with other egos to face a common enemy.

The ego's boundary for its sense of self gets enlarged to include all of the people on its side; it's no longer me vs. the enemy, but we vs. the enemy. Our competitiveness is what causes nations to spend on military forces and borders, instead of health care and education. We have prioritized death over life; we have space programs going to Mars, CEOs evergreening life-saving drugs, and hedge fund managers fighting over their billion-dollar stock bets, while people are getting evicted, struggling to make ends meet, and dying from starvation.

If there's no inward change, then any outward change will not work. We have seen the consequences of this from the implementation of Communism, where external change was imposed on a society where the individuals have not undergone an inner change. Communism was an ideology with the aim to establish a social structure rooted in equality—where there's no personal ownership and no social class, as opposed to the other regimes that polarized the social classes into the ruling and working (bourgeoisie vs. proletariat), which always resulted in conflict between the classes.

"The history of all hitherto existing society is the history of class struggles. ... In a word, oppressor and oppressed, stood in constant opposition to one another ... a fight that each time ended, either in a revolutionary reconstruction of society at large, or in the common ruin of the contending classes. ... The modern bourgeois society that has sprouted from the ruins of feudal society has not done away with class antagonisms. It has but established new classes, new conditions of oppression, new forms of struggle in place of the old ones. ... Society as a whole is more and more splitting up into two great hostile camps, into two great classes directly facing each other: Bourgeoisie and Proletariat."[13] (*The Communist Manifesto*)

The Communist ideology, in theory, was very similar to the spiritual teachings, where the aim was to relinquish our individual egos and align ourselves with the whole. But the problem of its implementation was that the people's inward state has not changed, so their psyche was still rooted in ego, in division. When people came into power in the Communist regime—they got corrupted by that power, and end up becoming the very thing that the Communist ideology opposed, which was the ruling class. So the society once again became divided. This is also what happened to various religions.

The original teaching of all religions was to realize that there is only one God, one Being, one Consciousness shared amongst all creations. But when the teachings became overly interpreted and in-stitutionalized—then people started to place their idea of God over the true God that is Conscious-ness. When that happens, people will pave the road to hell with their "good" intentions.

A well-known case of this is Mother Teresa. Her mission to spread Christianity overtook her mis-sion to serve those in need. So she siphoned the money she raised from charity to rich catholic churches instead of providing help to the patients in her hospital—which was whom the charity was intended for. Her hospitals ended up being known as the "houses of the dying." In one of her inter-views with Christopher Hitchens, she said, "I'm not a social worker. I don't do it for this reason. I do it for Christ. I do it for the Church." Mother Teresa was a Christian before she was a human being. Her opposition to abortion and birth control has led to over-population in various places that subse-quently trapped those people in a cycle of poverty and suffering.

When God is turned into a belief, then the teach-ings of God will get split into different religions with different ideologies and rituals, which have led to conflict between the religions that resulted in killing in the name of God. Any action derived from divisiveness is in direct contradiction to the original teaching which is that: all are one. If the religious devotees realized the teaching not merely on an intellectual level but on the level of their consciousness, then they would not be able to act from a place of divisiveness.

CHAPTER FOUR:
THE EGO'S CORE

LIVING IN ABSTRACTION

When two competitors are up against one another in a sports match, if the competitors realize that their performance depends on their opponent's performance, as they can only reach their best if their opponent can put up the necessary obstacles to allow them to do so. Then subsequently, they can also realize that an athlete is only as good as their opponent; if a star athlete wins against an amateur, then the win would not mean much, so an athlete's opponent is what defines the athlete; the opposing competitors are inseparable. Furthermore, the winner is also not separate from the loser because there is no winning without losing; they have to go together. If a competitor sees the competition's non-dual nature and realizes the winner is just as important as the loser, then the competitors can treat the competition as a play. As Lao Tzu wrote in *Tao Te Ching*:

"The best athlete wants his opponent at his best. ... The best leader follows the will of the people. All of them embody the virtue of non-competition. Not that they don't love to compete, but they do it in the spirit of play."[1]

But if a competitor's identity is invested in being the winner, then they would feel threatened from losing. In this case, the competition becomes a serious conflict. The egoic competitor has separated themself from their opponent; they no longer see their opponent as a human being, but instead, as an enemy and so deserving of any affliction.

The ego's separative perception has also separated the end from the means; the end result has become paramount while the means have become trivial. The ego can now justify using whatever means to achieve the goal, like cheating or injuring their opponent. The ego fails to see that the means are not separated from the end. If they injure their opponent, they will also destroy their identity as the winner, as their win now means nothing. And subsequently, they will also destroy their ability to compete because who will they play against if they have no willing opponent? The means and the end are one; more wars and more violence will not lead to peace. Only that which begins with peace can end with peace.

To end divisiveness within ourselves does not mean that we just yield to everything that we come into opposition with. It means that we first yield to the situation as it is, and then we act, because then we will be able to act from a place of harmony rather than a place of conflict. When we are inwardly peaceful, we are more easily attuned to our surroundings and thereby able to sense the right actions. Sometimes the situation may demand our opposition and aggression, but when we act in accordance with the universal flow, our actions will be powerful and sane.

In the book *Autobiography of a Yogi*, when Paramhansa Yogananda was conflicted in whether to kill a mosquito that had just bit him, his Guru Sri Yukteswar said:

> "Patanjali's meaning was the removal of DESIRE to kill. ... Man may be compelled to exterminate harmful creatures. He is not under similar compulsion to feel anger or animosity. All forms of life have equal right to the air of MAYA. The saint who uncovers the secret of creation will be in harmony with its countless bewildering expressions. All men may approach that understanding who curb the inner passion for destruction."[2]

When Paramhansa Yogananda asks whether one should sacrifice himself instead of killing an animal, Sri Yukteswar answers:

> "No; man's body is precious. It has the highest evolutionary value because of unique brain and spinal centers. These enable the advanced devotee to fully grasp and express the lofti-

est aspects of divinity. No lower form is so equipped. It is true that one incurs the debt of a minor sin if he is forced to kill an animal or any living thing. But the VEDAS teach that wanton loss of a human body is a serious transgression against the karmic law."[2]

When a situation calls for it, the soldier without ego can fight with humanity. An ego out of alignment with the universal flow may fight to feel superior. And since their superiority is derived externally, they will always need more, so they may fight far more than necessary. Furthermore, some parts of the ego may derive its superiority from being a dominant person, while other parts may derive it from being a virtuous person, but both are ideas—not actual—so there is conflict; the idea vs. the idea, and the idea vs. the actual.

When an animal kills another animal, the animal is never conflicted in its act. The animal has no hidden agenda; they are not killing for an ideology, not out of hate, and not to be superior. They are simply killing because there is a biological urge to kill, and once the deed is done, it is done. It leaves no psychological trace in the animal (there are exceptions, for example, dogs may develop some psychological capacity for negativity after being immersed in a human environment). The prey will fight for its survival to the best of its abilities, but when it knows it has been defeated, it will peacefully accept its end. No matter what the animal does, it is doing the right thing because it is in harmony and not in conflict.

This book is not suggesting that we should be like animals. The animal lacks the cerebral capacity to live in a different way, so it must kill to survive. Our cerebral capacity allows us to live more consciously than other life forms. Animals mostly live from their compulsions, so their environment is dictating their evolution—to a new life form with a higher cerebral capacity (like an ape to a human, as Darwin explained)—but we have the cerebral capacity to live far more consciously. Hence, our evolution is much more dependent on our consciousness rather than our environment. When our consciousness evolves—it will not be a lateral evolution from one form to another, but a vertical evolution from form to the formless, from human to the divine.

Our cerebral capacity allows us to discern between what is right from what is wrong—not mentally in the form of ideas—but we can sense it from our humanity. Our humanity does not need to be taught; it is intrinsic to our being. We don't want others to suffer what we ourselves don't want to suffer, so when we see a person or a creature in need of help, we naturally feel compassion and want to help. Our unconditioned compassion does not discriminate on any basis. Only when we try to act according to our mental model on what is right and wrong, then we discriminate; then we can justify our inhuman actions against those who hold different beliefs than us. When we become divisive, we lose our humanity and subsequently are capable of committing far worse acts than animals.

You cannot try to be humane or virtuous because in the process of trying, you are being a bunch of other things, so it is much more important to be aware of what you are from moment to moment, then you are living in reality and not in abstraction. From that awareness, your true nature will start to emerge. And your response to situations will flow effortlessly. In that response, there's a freshness to it, as you may be one thing in one moment and another in the next; you're no longer chained by rigid ideas, and you will be whatever is needed in each moment.

Then you are free, free from choice. Choice always implies conflict, one possibility vs. another. When there is only one possibility, then your energy is no longer in contradiction. In that serenity, there is real virtue; you no longer try to be virtuous because you have no concept of virtue. An animal, a tree, does not know virtue, and so it is virtuous. That's why Lao Tzu said: "superior virtue is not conscious of being virtuous, hence is truly virtuous."

The ego differentiates possibilities between right and wrong, good and bad, so it is always trying to figure out what to do in every situation. The situation gets more complex the more one thinks about it because it is all imaginary. This is why many people cannot stop thinking; they think that once they stop thinking, their lives will fall apart. What is it that is falling apart? Life is always on—it does not distinguish events between good and bad; chaos is part of life; death is part of life. Therefore, all the thinking about life is completely futile. The more you think about life, the more you get away from life, because you are increasingly living in abstraction.

Even if you had figured out what to do in every situation, you would not be able to do it when the situation comes, because what happens in your head is always different from reality. How many times have you carefully plotted out exactly what you were going to do, only to find out later that you ended up doing something completely different? An athlete meticulously plans out for each match, they think they are going to win, and they say they are going to win. As Conor McGregor says: "when I say something's going to happen, it's going to happen." But do they win every time? "Everybody has a plan until they get punched in the mouth." (Mike Tyson)

Every single generation, people always think that what they are doing now is the right thing—to correct the stupid things that people have done in the past. But only to recognize a few generations later that what they did turn out to be wrong again. And this will happen every time as long as we derive our rights and wrongs from our minds. We always think we know the right thing to do, but only to end up wrong in hindsight.

Many people believe they are a good person and is always willing to offer help to those in need. But when they actually encounter those situations in their daily life, they never offer help. So relinquish your need to know what to do all the time and start being more comfortable in a state of not knowing. Then you become more like water, like space in which you are very sensitive to life; you start to be able to sense what to do in each situation. This is your innate intuition that was previously veiled by conceptual thinking. Your space-like qualities will yield to all situations, which allows the situations to yield back and become helpful to you. When you're in tune with life, you become much more helpful to your surroundings. But when you're stuck in your mind, you become rigid and get into all sorts of problems. "When two great forces oppose each other, the victory will go to the one that knows how to yield. ... The hard and stiff will be broken. The soft and supple will prevail."[3] (Lao Tzu)

The ego will always oppose life, because the ego is intrinsically rigid while life is intrinsically transitory. The ego always wants permanency; if it has been living in luxury, it wants to continue living in luxury; if it has an attractive appearance, it wants to continue having that appearance; if it has a respectable social status, it wants to continue having that status; if it has a set of beliefs of how life should work, it wants life to work according to their beliefs. Thus, the ego lives in constant fear, fear of not getting what it want, fear of losing what it has, fear of others not treating it the way it expects to be treated, fear of life not working according to its beliefs on how life should work. "Change is the law of the universe. You can be a millionaire, or a pauper in an instant." (*Bhagavad Gita*)

EGO'S DEFENCE MECHANISMS

The root of ego's fear is some variation of not being enough, like being unworthy, inadequate, useless, helpless, alone, empty, nothing, etc. The feelings of unworthiness are sometimes induced by traumatic events early in one's life or by being repeatedly mistreated by others. To avoid the painful feelings, the ego tries to cling onto something in life—like a relationship, a job, an ideology—to find some sense of worth and meaning. But deep down, the ego knows that it will all be lost in time, because it sees that everything is in a constant state of decay.

The ego cannot face living in this world full of uncertainty, misery, meaninglessness, injustice, death, and brutality, so the ego separates itself from reality and escapes to a dream world where it is meaningful and predictable—and where it can be somebody who is important. This is why people like to immerse themselves in fictional works—where the world is typically exciting and predictable; the main character is important, and usually, everything works out in the end.

The ego will develop elaborate self-images and belief systems to construct its own dream world: "I will not share the fate of all these unfortunate people; I am rich, and my money will always protect me." "My life is not meaningless; I have accomplished so much more than everybody else." "I am a worthy husband; I have money, appearance, and personality, so my wife will never leave me." "I am not a nobody; I can do so and so better than everybody else; I am going to be a big deal soon, so people better respect me." "I am a good person, as I have followed all God's instructions, so God will always protect me and take care of me in heaven after I die."

To protect oneself from facing the harshness of reality, the ego needs to constantly fabricate wild rationalizations to keep its mental model of reality intact. When an ego that derives its identity in being a hard worker and believes that hard work should always dictate a person's success, sees that there are people who achieved far more success than himself effortlessly, the ego gets agitated and angry. The ego can't face the reality that maybe hard work doesn't always lead to success, so he starts to fabricate rationalizations like: "maybe they had connections or got lucky; I'm sure they will fail soon because they are lazy, and I will surpass them eventually."

When an ego that derives its identity in being a good-looking girl and believes that all of a girl's value is in her looks, sees her crush choosing to be with a girl less attractive than her, she gets distressed, and run to thoughts like: "maybe that girl is insanely rich; maybe he is intimidated to be with an attractive girl like me; good that he picked her because I could get a better guy anyways." She protected herself from facing the fact that maybe her looks aren't as important as she thinks.

An ego that sees herself to be a deeply unworthy person gets abused by her partner; she still chooses to remain in the relationship because she doesn't want to face the reality of her partner leaving, being unwanted, or of her partner not respecting her. So she escapes to rationalizations like: "he's just having a bad day; he's usually gentle towards me; I'm not going to find a better partner anyways." Therefore, the ego's unwillingness to face its own painful feelings has caused the kind of distorted thinking that further perpetuates its painful feelings by choosing to stay in an abusive relationship.

When an ego that derives its identity from being a "good" husband with a happy family and a loyal wife, goes through an experience where his wife decides to leave him for another man—he becomes deeply disturbed; he can't face the fact that he may not be as a "good" of a husband as he thinks.

So he escapes to thoughts like: "she was not good enough for me anyway; she is inconsiderate about my feelings; she is a slut." As a result, the ego constantly misinterprets situations and always acts from its own distorted perspective, which is likely to provoke the other's egoic reactions.

For example, when the husband accuses the wife of being a slut for leaving him with another man, the wife may get defensive and lash out back at the husband. Then the husband thinks that he was right in thinking that she is inconsiderate and thus not good enough for him. This is how the ego finds the justifications for its distorted perspectives; their own distortion-based actions are causing others to behave in line with their distorted perspective of the other. If a parent sees their child as a bad child and treats him that way, then the child is more likely to misbehave from that kind of treatment, which further reinforces the parent's perception of the child.

This book is not suggesting that the husband should always take the blame, and believe that his wife chose to leave him because he's not a "good" husband—maybe she just didn't want to continue the relationship, or maybe something else. There can be all sorts of reasons, but finding the "right" reason is not the concern, because the reason is always mind-made. It is much better to face reality as is. If the husband can examine himself without his distortions, then he may discover whether or not his behaviors were the cause of the separation. Such a discovery is a much more substantial change for the husband compared to him finding a wife who is more "loyal." And if the husband finds that his behaviors were not the problem, then he can simply deal with the fact that his wife is leaving, instead of generating all that story on the reason why she left, because then the situation would be much less dramatic.

The label "slut" is a mental fabrication. Even if the wife did do something that is typically looked down upon in society, like cheating or being promiscuous, then the husband can still deal with the situation non-reactively. The husband's conscious behavior may even help the wife to disidentify from her ego and examine her own behavior, which is a much better outcome compared to an angry confrontation that causes the wife to further identify with her ego—which will only lead to more negative drama.

When the ego's root pain gets disturbed, that pain spawns into new variants in response to different situations; like sorrow in response to losing a loved one; guilt in response to having realized you've done something that you shouldn't have done; jealousy in response to seeing your wife flirting with other people; despair in response to having nothing to look forward to; and embarrassment in response to doing or saying something stupid in front of others.

The ego also develops other emotions like anger, hatred, and superiority to hide all its unworthiness, and will create new self-images to justify those emotions: "I should be angry; because I'm smart and you're an idiot; because I'm right and you're wrong; because I'm the victim and you're discriminating against me." "I hate this guy; he is so egotistical; he is so annoying; who the f*ck does he think he is talking to me like that; he always acts like he is better than me; I hope he fails at whatever he is doing; just watch I will surpass him one day." "That guy used to talk down to me all the time, and now I'm more successful than him, haha." "Five years ago, that girl left me for someone else, and now she wishes she could be with me because my life is way better than hers, serves her right for leaving me." As the emotions become more rooted in different self-images, thoughts, and memories, this mixture of psychological processes starts to form distinct patterns in the mind —which can act as independent entities. This is how some of the mental entities are formed.

The ego thinks that its protective entities can shield itself from its unworthiness, but on the contrary, they only exacerbate them. Because its superiority persona can come off as very repulsive to others—which in turn causes the ego more isolation, the ego can also get embarrassed by its arrogant, angry and hateful behaviors, which then lead the ego to try to disguise those behaviors by creating more self-images like a humble, calm or loving person.

To maintain its facade of images, the ego constantly needs approval from others. Such approval-seeking behavior is often what causes disrespectful behaviors toward the ego—which disturbs the ego more—and subsequently further reinforces the ego's belief of being unworthy. This is how the cycle of a belief creating the situation, and then the situation in turn further reinforcing the belief, is formed; it's a self-reinforcing delusion. As Jeff Foster said: "The more you try to fix it, the more you reinforce the belief that it's broken."

When the ego gets embarrassed by its approval-seeking behavior—it creates even more self-images like a person that don't care about what others think. However, the ego still secretly wants others' approval, so it becomes more cunning and subtle in its approach. The ego will continue this back-and-forth of image creation and behavior tuning until it feels like it has sufficiently deceived everyone, including itself. Eventually, the ego will have developed a network of images and emotions that acts as a complex algorithm to govern its every action. This algorithm is extremely energy-draining as it constantly needs to ensure that it pleases everyone in every social situation.

The ego may feel like it was successful in becoming a worthy person, but deep down, it knows there are inconsistencies in its identity, because does a person who is truly worthy need to make all this effort? The ego's internal inconsistencies will express themselves through its inauthenticity, and hence, other people can always sense it. People will (sometimes unknowingly) stirrup the ego's hidden pain—by jabbing at its phony images: "You are not as great as you think you are; why you always f*ck things up? You're never gonna amount to much; you're an arrogant prick; you're a loser; you're ugly; you're an idiot; I forgot to invite you; I don't like you because of your race, status, appearance, etc." This is how people get offended, and what people call getting "triggered" or getting their "buttons" pushed, their "trigger" or "button" is their self-image.

Without the self-image, what exactly would be offended? Would the body by itself react to the words? If you had lost all your memory, then the insult would simply pass through you. But when I have an image of myself being a smart person, and then somebody comes along and calls me an idiot, then I would be offended. Because I don't want others to think of me as an idiot; I want to protect that image; that image is me.

If our self-images are not involved in a disagreement, then we can collaborate with the other to discover the truth. We can investigate the situation and find the evidence to support our argument. If we still can't come to a consensus after some time, then we can just agree to disagree. However, if both of us are completely attached to our mental positions, then the dispute can only get more hostile. No one is willing to give up their position, as our sense of self is completely derived from being right and making the other wrong. To admit defeat feels like dying to the ego, so we end up defending ourselves and attacking others as if our lives depended on it.

EMOTIONAL PAIN

A person with many self-images to defend will often misinterpret things and get triggered with the slightest remark. And the degree of their identification to their self-images will be expressed through the intensity of their emotional reactions —a very intense emotional reaction can exhibit itself either outwardly in the form of explosive anger or inwardly in the form of a mental shut down.

If we are willing to simply face our pain, then we wouldn't have to waste all of our energy protecting it. But we are unwilling to face it because it gets so uncomfortable when we get near it, so we want to get as far away from it as possible. This is why most of us can't stand solitude; we need to constantly distract ourselves with social media, sex, drugs, work, games, parties, and vacations so our pains can remain dormant.

We will also avoid people, places, and activities that can evoke our pain. Hence, our lives have become dull and repetitive as we go through each day with the same job, the same acquaintances, and the same routines. The more we neglect our pain, the more we are at the mercy of it. Eventually, our entire life and personality are revolved around escaping our pain. And relationships in society have become shallow as a result, because everyone is walking on eggshells in order to avoid evoking everyone else's pain. We all stick to "safe" topics like the weather, food, and vacations, and we all wear a happy mask, so others do not see our true feelings.

> "If you do not want to deal with the pain at its core, then what you do to avoid it had better work. If you are hiding yourself in a busy social life, then anything anyone does that challenges your self-esteem, such as not inviting you to an event, will cause you to feel the pain. … How does that generate pain? It is because deep inside there is pain that you have not processed. Your attempt to avoid this pain has created layer upon layer of sensitivities that are all linked to the hidden pain.

> … At the core there is the pain. Then, in order to avoid the pain, you try to stay busy with friends and hide in their acceptance. That is the first layer out. Then, in order to assure your acceptance, you try to present yourself a certain way so that you can win friends and influence people. That is another layer out. Each layer is attached to the original pain. This is why simple, everyday interactions can affect

you so much. If the core pain was not the motivation behind proving yourself each day, what people say would not affect you. But since avoiding the core pain is why you're trying to prove yourself, you end up bringing the potential for pain into everything that happens. You end up so sensitive that you are unable to live in this world without getting hurt. ... If you watch carefully, you will see that even simple interactions often cause some degree of pain, insecurity, or general disturbance."[4] (Michael A. Singer, *The Untethered Soul*)

The ego thinks that it can get rid of its pain by escaping or repressing it, but it will only perpetuate it. Every time our pain gets stirred, we unconsciously contract ourselves to stop the uncomfortable feelings from overwhelming our body, and over time our bodies will be filled with layers upon layers of unprocessed emotional pain. This dense mass of emotional pain within the body is what Eckhart Tolle calls the pain-body. In some cases, a very heavy pain-body can cause physical illnesses within the body.

The pain-body remains dormant in our body when we are distracted, but periodically it bubbles up into the surface, sometimes triggered by phrases or imagery in our thoughts or the external situation. From a sensational perspective, the pain kind of feels like a knot in the heart area, and when the pain is very intense, it can feel like a heavy stone on the chest. In terms of emotional state, a mild pain-body can feel like boredom and a heavy pain-body can feel like depression.

When our pain-body becomes active, it will try to seek situations to reinvigorate the identities that are associated with the pain, so its stored negativity can have an outlet. For example, an angry ego will go around and look for a reason to lash out; the ego wants to find those who also have a lot of stored anger so that its own anger can be reciprocated. This is how fights and disputes happen. If one party in the dispute has no stored anger, then the insults will have nothing to stirrup, and so it will just flow past them. The calm victim will simply refuse to participate in the dispute and yield to the other's aggression. When the perpetrator finds that their aggression is not resisted, they may get annoyed for a bit, but eventually, their own anger will defuse.

If the pain-body cannot find any external situation to vent its stored negativity, then it will take over your mind and continuously indulge itself in negative thought patterns, like thinking about how messed up your life is or how much you hate so and so.

"The pain-body wants to survive, just like every other entity in existence, and it can only survive if it gets you to unconsciously identify with it. It can then rise up, take you over, 'become you,' and live through you. It needs to get its 'food' through you. It will feed on any experience that resonates with its own kind of energy, anything that creates further pain in whatever form: anger, destructiveness, hatred, grief, emotional drama, violence, and even illness. So the pain-body, when it has taken you over, will create a situation in your life that reflects back its own energy frequency for it to feed on. Pain can only feed on pain. Pain cannot feed on joy. It finds it quite indigestible.

Once the pain-body has taken you over, you want more pain. You become a victim or a perpetrator. You want to inflict pain, or you want to suffer pain, or both."[5] (Eckhart Tolle, *The Power of Now*)

THE CONTRADICTORY NATURE OF THE EGO

The ego ultimately wants to become all-powerful and infinite so it can completely eradicate its sense of lack, but its very methodology prevents the goal. The ego can only grow incrementally, and an incremental process can never lead to infinity. The ego first identifies itself as a student, then it wants to get hired so it can become an employee, then a distinguished employee, then a CEO, then a president, then a trillionaire, then the ruler of the galaxy, and so on. The ego also latches onto material possessions, "my house, my car, my money, my companies, my employees, mine, mine, mine..."

As the ego's conceptual body grows, its boundary for its sense of self also grows; the boundary may start with the physical body, then it includes the family, then the classmates, then the company, then a sports team, then a nation, and so on. The ego is always in a state of becoming, of wanting, but never in a state of arrival. And no matter how grand its sense of self has become, it's still insignificant compared to the infinite universe, so why set a boundary on the self at all? Because the ego's existence is derived from the boundary between itself and others.

The ego does not see that its own cessation is actually what it longs for the most. Deep down, the ego wants to remove the boundary between itself and others. That's why it's always trying to unite with something other than itself—either physically in sex, emotionally in an intimate relationship, or spiritually in prayer or meditation. That's also why people partake in dangerous activities, like mountain climbing and wingsuit flying—during those activities, all of their attention is forced to be in the present moment because otherwise, it would be fatal. Such experiences simulate a near-death experience where you have completely accepted your end and thereby relinquished all psychological control. When people's attention is removed from their mind, then their past identity ends, and at that moment, ecstasy emerges. People falsely attribute ecstasy to activities or drugs, but it's actually the cessation of the ego.

The problem with seeking oneness in experiences is that all forms are intrinsically dualistic. Sex may momentarily unite two bodies and provide people with a sense of unity. But a man and a woman can never become one. The more you try to unite them, the more problem ensues, because you are trying to develop commonality on energies that are polar opposites. Life is a play of dualities; if the polar energies become too similar, then the very force that attracts them will be gone. In the dimension of form, two can never become one, so if you are chasing a sense of oneness from experiences, then you will just become more dependent on an external stimuli. Instead of finding liberation from oneness, you have found more bondage.

The ego also does not see the contradiction of its purpose. The ego wants to destroy the other so it can be regarded as better than others. But what the ego does not realize is that that which it's constantly trying to destroy—the other, the enemy—is the very thing that sustains its own existence; without the existence of the other—its own existence would also end.

A student whose ego derives its identity from being a top performer in the class cannot exist without all the other students that had performed worse. If every student's performance were just as good as the top student, then that student would no longer be regarded as the top performer, and subsequently, its ego would vanish. Similarly, an ego that derives its identity from its political ideology cannot exist if there are no opposing ideologies. An ego needs comparison to exist: "I am smarter than you; I have more money than you; my ideology is more correct than yours; I am better than you." Therefore, the ego will never achieve its purpose because it will always find something to oppose. Even if there are no actual enemies, the ego will just invent one, like: "secret societies," "rich elitists," "ignorant masses," and so on. There is no such thing as a "rich elitist," there are only individuals like you and me; when the ego labels the other, it dehumanizes the other, so it can turn off its humanity when it hates and destroys the other.

Another thing the ego does not recognize is that the qualities that it despises the most in others are often the very qualities that are the most prominent in itself. Because the ego can only despise what it knows, it can only know that which is already within itself. This is why the ego tends to attract the very people it hates into its surroundings. If I don't understand the psyche of a serial killer, then I may be disgusted by their actions. But I do not obsessively hate serial killers every day because I cannot relate to them. So there's more curiosity than hatred. However, if I'm very attention-seeking, then I know how attention-seekers think; I know they're fake, so I obsessively hate them. I also want to be acknowledged as different from them—and that can't happen unless there's a contrast, so I have unknowingly surrounded myself with attention-seekers, because then I can act in such a way as to stand out from them.

If you observe people carefully, you will find that the type of things that they complain about are typically the very things that they commit themselves, and the kinds of people that they complain about usually make up the majority of their social circle.

When you judge another on some standard, you are simultaneously judging yourself as well. And the hatred that you direct toward the other—for not measuring up—is also directed towards yourself, because no one can measure up to an abstract standard 100% of the time. Regardless of how the hatred is directed, it is still within you, so when you judge, you are becoming more judgemental and hateful, which makes you more contemptible. That's why Jesus said: "do not judge, or you too will be judged."[6]

You may think that you are a "good" person—unlike the others you judge—but you may need to break the standard sooner or later, so you need to constantly restrain yourself as not to look like a hypocrite. Hence, you have become rigid, which actually breeds hypocrisy and vileness. Also, because you believed that you are "good," you end up becoming unwilling to face the bad deeds that you yourself commit. So you get defensive or embarrassed when others call you out on it, and you end up further perpetuating your vileness as a result. As Jesus said: "why do you look at the speck of sawdust in your brother's eye and pay no attention to the plank in your own eye?"[7]

When we are always blaming others, we can never solve any problem. From a middle or low-class perspective, we think that the rich are the problem. We say why are they hoarding billions of dollars when most of the world is in poverty and food insecure? But at the same time, we want other people to give us high-income jobs so that we can live a more comfortable life; do we not see our contradiction? Who do we think are the people that can give us those jobs? Is it not the rich? If we can't blame them, maybe we can blame the corrupted politicians who have rigged the system to favour the rich. Again, where do we think those politicians come from? They didn't come from outer space. We voted them there. Also, their mentality is developed by the kind of society that we have created. If we create a competitive society, then the people will be corrupted; it doesn't matter which political party gets voted into the office or which individual makes it to the top.

When we believe that the rich are bad and get stuck on quotes like: "the love of money is the root of all evil," then we are sabotaging our own success. Because our unconscious guilt to be the one of the rich will cause our mind to avoid the opportunities that can generate real wealth. We become risk-averse when we adopt an "honest hard-worker" or a scarcity mentality, because we want to avoid our fears or do things the "right" way, so we stick to what we know and miss all the other possibilities. We are also sabotaging ourselves when we get hateful of others' success; we don't want to acknowledge them being better than us, so we brush them off as being lucky. We will avoid learning from them as a result.

A common misconception that we have about the rich is that they just have billions of dollars lying around to spend; we imagine them to have a lavish lifestyle and are happy all the time, so we feel left out or diminished as a result. Billionaires don't have billions of cash lying around. It's their net worth that shows the billions; it's how much their stocks are valued. If they convert all their stocks to cash, then they have to sell, which would not only tank their stock price (especially if they do it in a short period) but that they would also lose ownership of their company—which is far more valuable to them. And what is the value of their money if they have nothing substantial to buy? If you were the richest person a couple of millennia ago, then you would not live any more lavishly than pretty much anybody alive today. Also, most billionaires are not interested in living fancily—they are much more focused on making their vision come true. Many have opted to donate their entire wealth to charity.

When we equate things like a lavish lifestyle to happiness, then we have made our happiness into an emotion, because it comes from comparison. When we live better than we did yesterday, or if we make more money than our friends, then we are happy. A beggar can have the happiest day of his life if offered a job, while a billionaire can feel worse if they only made $100 million from a deal. When you ask most people whether they would rather make $80k, but all their friends make $100k or make $60k, and all of their friends make $40k, they would choose the latter. It is this kind of mentality that has kept the collective wages low because people don't like the poorer ones surpassing them, so they would rather put their energy into keeping them down rather than focusing on raising everyone's wealth.

When happiness comes from your very being, then it is no longer an emotion; it is not happiness in opposition to misery; it is the background of all emotions. When happiness is caught up in duality, then sooner or later, it will swing the other way, because you cannot have the crest without the trough. Even if you are living the most lavish lifestyle, you will eventually get sick of it.

All experiences will eventually adjust to your natural state. That's why some people can be happy in prison, while others can be miserable in a mansion. As Dalai Lama wrote in *The Art of Happiness*: "Happiness is determined more by one's state of mind than by external events."[8] "He is richest who is content with the least, for content is the wealth of nature." (Socrates)

From an upper-class perspective, we think that the masses are the problem; we think they are ignorant, unskilled, and contribute nothing to the economy while asking for handouts. If there are robots that can do a better job than them with less cost, then why do we bother with them? It is this kind of thinking that has made people afraid of technology. People should welcome automation as it can free them from menial tasks so that they can enjoy life as human beings. But instead, people are resisting automation. This is because we have commodified human beings, so people have to compete with robots. Human beings can never win against machines. Eventually, we will be surpassed by A.I. even in the most intelligent tasks. It is only at that point that perhaps people start to question what it really means to be human.

If we destroy the masses, then what good is our service if there's no one who can afford it? And who are we serving if it's not the masses? What is the point of crushing all of our competitors and amassing all of that wealth, if all we have left to buy are our own crappy products? When a company completely dominates the market, then the quality of their service will inevitably drop, because when there's no alternative service, there's also no incentive for excellence. That's why the government typically gets outdone by the private sector in similar services. The monopoly companies still have some competition. If Google were to falter, people could switch to another search engine like Bing. But people cannot switch services provided by the government.

Life is only meaningful when we make others happy. There's only so much pleasure that we can enjoy by ourselves. Eventually, we have to align with our innate compassion and find real happiness from serving others. Thus, neither the ruling nor the working class needs to blame the other. Instead, we can recognize the symbiotic relationship that we have with the other. As long as we think the problem is out there, there will never be any substantial change. Only when we look within —and see our own thorn—before any transformation can happen within and without. As Jiddu Krishnamurti wrote in *The First and Last Freedom*:

> "In order to transform the world about us, with its misery, wars, unemployment, starvation, class divisions and utter confusion, there must be a transformation in ourselves. The revolution must begin within oneself – but not according to any belief or ideology, because revolution based on an idea, or in conformity to a particular pattern, is obviously no revolution at all. To bring about a fundamental revolution in oneself, one must understand the whole process of one's thought and feeling in relationship. That is the only solution to all our problems – not to have more disciplines, more

beliefs, more ideologies and more teachers. If we can understand ourselves as we are from moment to moment without the process of accumulation, then we shall see how there comes a tranquillity that is not a product of the mind, a tranquillity that is neither imagined nor cultivated; and only in that state of tranquillity can there be creativeness."[9]

"Be the change that you wish to see in the world." (Mahatma Gandhi)

CHAPTER FIVE: LIBERATION

SELF-INQUIRY

How can we go about examining ourselves? How can we be free from this complex psychological disorder that is the ego? First of all, do we even want to be free of it?

When life is happening just the way we want, when we got a good job, a good family, and our business are doing great. Then we live very superficially and arrogantly; we become ignorant of our divisiveness and delusions. We treat this spiritual stuff as extracurricular, as entertainment, as an interesting idea to play around with in our heads. This stuff is not taught in our schools, and our parents and friends don't talk about it. Everybody else gets angry, hateful, and divisive, so why should we deal with our conditioning?

When we are so identified as the ego, then we are not really concerned about our conditioning because we want what the ego wants more than anything else. We strongly believe that fulfilling our ego's desires will bring us our long-awaited happiness, even if our past experiences indicate otherwise. So we continue to wait for our next soulmate, for our next big success, and even if we have waited for lifetimes—we still go along with it. After all, the ego has been helpful so far; it has got us good grades, a secure job, so why should we want to get rid of it? For those people, they will not be concerned with their conditioning; they most likely would have never even opened this kind of book.

However, reality rarely conforms to any delusion for long. Sooner or later, it will start cracking the ego's fragile shell—as things will go wrong. We may lose our job, lose our loved ones, or contract a serious disease—it is only then that we really start to look within ourselves. As Friedrich Nietzsche said: "There are no beautiful surfaces without a terrible depth." So for many people, suffering is their only teacher because a mere intellectual grasp of the ego will not typically bring about sub-stantial change. Only when there is intense suffer-ing—can people be brought to a much deeper place of seeing. A Zen master once told a man seeking liberation: "come back and see me when you want enlightenment as bad as you wanted air."

We must actually see the ego within us—see its parasitic and pathological nature—and only then can we start to really understand its workings and subsequently be free from it. We can only do that when we inquire deeply into ourselves. Also, we must be extremely honest with ourselves and be clear on our motives during our inquiry. Are we genuinely interested in understanding ourselves? Or is it because of something else?

If we are inquiring into ourselves with a motive, either to get something at the end of it—like enlightenment, happiness, or because somebody else said it's important—then we are no longer inquiring. Because our inquiry is censored by the desires of our past or by the authority of another. We also cannot learn about ourselves from someone else like a psychologist or a philosopher, because otherwise, we are learning about their mind—not our own mind.

Therefore, we must stand alone and be completely naked during our self-inquiry, without our past —whether it's a doctrine we have adopted since childhood, or something we learned yesterday. "[The] authority of yesterday is as destructive as the authority of a thousand years"[1] (Jiddu Krishnamurti). When we remain alone—we become fresh and untainted by memory; only in such a state can genuine learning take place.

> "Understanding is not an intellectual process. Accumulating knowledge about yourself and learning about yourself are two different things ... Learning about yourself is not like learning a language ... knowledge is always in the past... But if you are learning all the time, learning every minute ... then you will find that learning is a constant movement without

the past.

If you say you will learn gradually about yourself, adding more and more, little by little, you are not studying yourself now as you are but through acquired knowledge. Learning implies a great sensitivity. There is no sensitivity if there is an idea, which is of the past, dominating the present. Then the mind is no longer quick, pliable, alert. ... To understand anything you must live with it, you must observe it, you must know all its content, its nature, its structure, its movement. Have you ever tried living with yourself? If so, you will begin to see that yourself is not a static state, it is a fresh living thing. And to live with a living thing your mind must also be alive. And it cannot be alive if it is caught in opinions, judgements and values."[2] (Jiddu Krishnamurti, *Freedom From the Known*)

There are many of us who, despite having clearly seen the destructiveness of our ego and how it makes us suffer, but are still unwilling to let it go. This is because our competitive culture has deeply ingrained us in the belief that happiness and success are ultimately mutually exclusive. Thus, even though the ego causes us to suffer, however, we still think it's a necessary part of success.

MISCONCEP-TIONS OF THE EGO

We see successful egos all over society; there are many famous people who come off as extremely egoistical in the media. And those people tend to tout how important it is to think highly of yourself and believe in how great you're going to become and how much you are going to achieve. Some examples include Muhammad Ali's "I'll show you how great I am" speech and Michael Jordan's "there's no 'I' in team, but there's an 'I' in win" quote. We often hear famous artists and athletes like Kanye West, Drake, Conor McGregor, and Le-Bron James refer to themselves as the GOAT or God.

Successful people also tend to say that success can only come from constant striving: "The only thing that I see that is distinctly different about me is I'm not afraid to die on a treadmill" (Will Smith). "I can't relate to lazy people. We don't speak the same language" (Kobe Bryant). "Work like hell. I mean you just have to put in 80 to 100 hour weeks every week" (Elon Musk). When we see that, we tend to attribute their success to their belief systems and stressful work style, but in reality, their egoic mindset is not the contributor to those people's successes; what they think they are doing and what they actually experience subjectively are two different things. As Ryan Holiday wrote in his book *Ego Is the Enemy*:

> "We see risk-taking swagger and successful people in the media, and eager for our own successes, try to reverse engineer the right attitude, the right pose. ... We intuit a causal relationship that isn't there. We assume the symptoms of success are the same as success itself—and in our naiveté, confuse the byproduct with the cause. Sure, ego has worked for some. Many of history's most famous men and women were notoriously egotistical. But so were many of its greatest failures. Far more of them, in fact. ... No one is truly successful because they are delusional, self-absorbed, or disconnected. Even if these traits are correlated or associated with certain well-known individuals, so are a few others: addiction, abuse (of themselves and others), depression, mania. In fact, what we see when we study these people is that they did their best work in the moments when they fought back against these impulses, disorders,

and flaws. Only when free of ego and baggage can anyone perform to their utmost."[3]

Phil Jackson is arguably the greatest coach in the NBA—winning 11 rings as a coach, which is more than any other coach in professional sports history. The environment that he worked at is filled with some of the most egotistical people on earth. The athletes and especially the stars are known to boast about their abilities and accomplishments. He personally coached some of them, like Michael Jordan, Shaquille O'Neal, and Kobe Bryant. So even Phil Jackson—the most successful coach in one of the most ego dominated industries—recognized that true success ultimately lies in the relinquishment of our egos and aligning ourselves to the whole, as he wrote in his book *Eleven Rings*:

> "As a leader your job is to do everything in your power to create the perfect conditions for success by benching your ego and inspiring your team to play the game the right way. But at some point, you need to let go and turn yourself over to the basketball gods. The soul of success is surrendering to what is."[4]

When the ego is involved in pursuing a goal, then it will constantly waste your energy on comparison with others and judging yourself based on how close you have gotten to your destination. When your energy is not aligned with the moment-to-moment living, then your actions will constantly be offbeat. You will feel like swimming against the stream, and your journey becomes much longer and also very painful as a result. A Zen master once said: "when you have one eye on the goal, you only have one eye on the path."

"To the untrained eye ego-climbing and selfless climbing may appear identical. Both kinds of climbers place one foot in front of the other. Both breathe in and out at the same rate. Both stop when tired. Both go forward when rested. But what a difference! The ego-climber is like an instrument that's out of adjustment. He puts his foot down an instant too soon or too late. He's likely to miss a beautiful passage of sunlight through the trees. He goes on when the sloppiness of his step shows he's tired. He rests at odd times. He looks up the trail trying to see what's ahead even when he knows what's ahead because he just looked a second before. He goes too fast or too slow for the conditions and when he talks his talk is forever about somewhere else, something else. He's here but he's not here. He rejects the here, is unhappy with it, wants to be farther up the trail but when he gets there will be just as unhappy because then it will be 'here.' What he's looking for, what he wants, is all around him, but he doesn't want that because it is all around him. Every step's an effort, both physically and spiritually, because he imagines his goal to be external and distant."[5] (Robert M. Pirsig, *Zen and the Art of Motorcycle Maintenance*)

The times when people have delivered their greatest performances, were usually when they were so engaged in the moment that they have completely lost themselves. It's almost like they are watching the game playing itself; they—the doer of actions —have vanished. This is the state of being in the flow or in the zone that many athletes describe. This is also what Lao Tzu calls the state of "non-action," as he said: "when nothing is done, nothing is left undone."[6]

You may have experienced this as well, if there was an exam that you have crammed hard for, but you still have performance anxiety because of the time restraint and the exam's importance. However, when the exam starts, all of your anxiety suddenly ends; there are no thoughts about how well you were going to do, how the grade may affect your future, etc. You were forced to tune out everything except the question in front of you, and you have become completely serene. The answers are flowing effortlessly from your mind, not in the form of noisy thoughts, but more like a thoughtless knowing. After the exam, your past identity comes back. You start to imagine how your performance may affect your future, and your mind starts to chat again.

When people are stuck in ego mode, you can

feel the atmosphere getting tense. The situations have become very cumbersome to deal with, and you feel like you have to slog through everything. When people's egos are gone, the situations become much lighter and lively. You feel like you're flowing through things effortlessly.

The ego's goals are often trap goals, you may feel excited about them at first, but after some time, you don't know why you're caught up in them. You know a goal comes from the ego when you feel suffocated by it. And after finally reaching it, you don't feel significantly different. This is why people always need to be motivated to do something. If you are genuinely interested in the activity, then you wouldn't need to pump yourself up with reasons to do it. As Elon Musk said: "If you need inspiring words, you should not do it." A joyful activity needs no reason to justify itself. Only a fabricated purpose needs to justify its existence: "I'm going to accomplish this or that so I can save the planet, so I can save humanity."

All purposes are ultimately fabricated. There is no purpose in life. Because a purpose can be fulfilled sooner or later, then what's next after that? Does life suddenly cease once the purpose is fulfilled? The moment-to-moment existence is the purpose. The goal is already in the means. "We do not exist for the sake of something else. We exist for the sake of ourselves."[7] (Shunryu Suzuki)

"You do not play a sonata *in order* to reach the final chord, and if the meanings of things were simply in ends, composers would write nothing but finales."[8] (Alan Watts)

Most people want to become so-called great to justify their existence, so other people can stop criticizing them. What they end up getting is the exact opposite; they only get more criticisms the greater they become. When you are a nobody, nobody's going to criticize you—only when you are well-known, then people will start criticizing. Just take a look at the celebrities in recent times, whether you are LeBron James—who is frequently regarded as the GOAT in the NBA—or Floyd Mayweather—who remains undefeated in boxing—or the president of the United States. No matter how much those individuals seem to have accomplished, there are still intense criticisms everywhere towards them. The more you accomplish, the more people will nitpick at you.

So if you want "greatness" just to escape your innate fear of being inadequate, then it will surely backfire, as it will only exacerbate that fear. Also, to achieve something "great" will always be an idea, a mental fabrication, and you can never achieve anything "great" if you don't take care of the present moment; see how far you can go if you don't take a breath in the now. As Phil Jackson wrote:

"Most of us spend the bulk of our time caught up in thoughts of the past or the future—which can be dangerous if your job is winning basketball games. Basketball takes place at such a lightning pace that it's easy to make mistakes and get obsessed with what just happened or what might happen next, which distracts you from the only thing that really matters—this very moment."[9]

Have you ever noticed that when you are really ecstatic, you have never once thought about the purpose? Only when you're functioning through the ego, then you start to care about what can be accomplished in the end. "When you do things from your soul, you feel a river moving in you, a joy." (Rumi)

"When you seek power and control over other people, you waste energy. When you seek money or power for the sake of the ego, you spend energy chasing the illusion of happiness instead of enjoying happiness in the moment. When you seek money for personal gain only, you cut off the flow of energy to yourself, and interfere with the expression of nature's intelligence. But when your actions are motivated by love, there is no waste of energy. When your actions are motivated by love, your energy multiplies and accumulates — and the surplus energy you gather and enjoy can be channeled to create anything that you want, including unlimited wealth."[10] (Deepak Chopra, *The Seven Spiritual Laws of Success*)

One misconception that most people have about the ego is that they think it's some kind of arrogance. Ego does not always come in the form of arrogance. Some ego can derive its sense of self from being a humble, spiritual, or even ego-less person. Our identity by itself as factual knowledge is not the problem. We need a name, a role, so other people can identify us to accomplish practical tasks. We need an outward identity to function in society, but inwardly, why do we need an identity?

When you are working as a waiter in a diner, you can fulfill the responsibilities of that role in that setting. But you don't need to identify yourself as a waiter to the degree that you start to feel inadequate when interacting with others who have a "superior" role. Similarly, if you are a CEO, then you can perform your role in the workplace, but you don't need to have a sense of superiority over others due to your role.

If we know our identity as merely a representation of us, then it's fine, but when we take our identity to be us, then the problem starts. Because then things become personal: "my thoughts, my identity, my problems, my story, my self-centredness, my loneliness." Nothing in existence is personal; self-centredness and loneliness are universal phenomenons. Your anger is humanity's anger; just as it is not American or Chinese anger, it is not yours or my anger.

BREAKING
IDENTIFICATION

To see how you are entangled to your identity, you can spend some time alone—where you stop all activity—and instead just observe your mental and emotional state. But not observing with an agenda to understand, judge or fix, because then you will just build another unobserved thought entity that will derive its identity on how much you can diminish the ego. The voice that wants to destroy the ego is the ego. However, if you do catch yourself observing with an agenda, then just notice that as another thought process, and continue on observing instead of adding further layers of agenda.

When you first start to be alone with your mind, you may find that it can be quite difficult, because your mind may start shouting: "this is a waste of time; this is so boring; let's think about something; let's do something." You find that your attention gets continuously pulled into one thought pattern after another, as you keep thinking about the ways you can be successful, the person you hate, why you were right on that argument the other day, and so on.

When you get to know more about your mind, you may become quite disturbed by its content. As there can be various voices going on within your mind all the time; not only are there your voice, but other people's voices as well—arising from your memories and projections. Such voices are typically accompanied by imageries, feelings, and sensations—pretty much like a dream movie playing. Some voices can get very repetitive—saying the same things over and over again: "I'm not good enough, I've accomplished more than so and so, I'm right, and they are wrong." The voices can also argue back and forth with each other and contradict each other all the time: "I shouldn't have done that; no, I should have been doing that way sooner. This is the way it is; no, that is how it is."

If you manage to remain only as the witness to your psychological process, rather than being continuously involved with them. Then a gap can start to open up between you and your thoughts, as you may notice that you're more still while your thoughts are happening. And although you are still pulled into thoughts sometimes. However, there are more frequent moments when you regain awareness—where you once again notice that you are the one simply observing your thoughts.

In a heated argument, when your awareness is

completely absorbed in your mental position and anger, then you are completely oblivious to your surroundings. But after some time, you may realize how involved you got in the argument. When that happens, your mental and emotional involvement suddenly subsides, then your awareness expands. You are aware of your surroundings and the context of the situation again; this is an example of how awareness is regained.

As you remain as the impartial witness to your experiences, your involvement and reactivity to situations will naturally drop. And it is good to practice observing yourself alone, because it is much easier to still your attention when you are not engaged in demanding activities. The watching of your mental and emotional state is commonly known as meditation in various spiritual or religious practices.

Meditation can start off being a practice or a technique, and so it can feel like it needs effort. This is primarily because most of us have been conditioned to paying attention outwardly rather than paying attention inwardly. But after some time of sinking the attention back to itself, you will eventually discover that you are the very attention itself. So it no longer takes any effort to be conscious, and you can engage in various activities without losing your true nature; fighting, thinking, and sleeping will not interrupt your meditation.

The true meaning of self-consciousness is being conscious of consciousness, because the true self is consciousness and not ego. Most people only pay attention to their self-image, so they live in perpetual anxiety.

You do not need to live in isolation to become liberated. Nevertheless, it may help at the beginning when your attention is very erratic. However, even if you are partaking in activities, you can still conduct yourself consciously, because there's no distance between you and consciousness. And ultimately, we do not exist in isolation; we exist in relationships. Even if you go live in a cave, you will still need to transact with the environment, and your past may still dominate your mind. So you need to be conscious of yourself every moment. It is often in the most challenging situations; your deepest conditioning starts to reveal itself. "The choice is always before you: to *respond consciously* to the present; or to *react compulsively* to it. There is a vast difference between the two. And it can make the world of a difference."[11] (Sadhguru)

When you hear the news of your friend getting a good job offer, look at how your thoughts race to the job you currently hold, so your mind can reassess your standing in relation to their new position. When someone criticizes you, look at how your mind exaggerates the situation by making up a bunch of reasons, like why that person is stupid and why you're justified in your behaviors. A fact may be "he disagreed with me," but your mind may say, "how dare he disagree with me? Does he not know who I am? I'm way more accomplished than him." You can start to see how your mind distorts reality. When you act on such distortions, you may end up completely ignoring the other's argument. As a result, you are more likely to make mistakes. When you are proven wrong after your display of arrogance, you get severely embarrassed. This is how your conditioning makes you suffer.

It will take a bit of time to disentangle ourselves from our habits, because our patterns of egoic thinking and feeling were rooted so deeply into us, as we have acted out such patterns for years and years. The amount of time it will take to realize the reality beyond our ego will depend on the individual; some may recognize their true nature instantly, while others may take lifetimes. But don't think that time is what liberates you. The "you" that needs time is the false you—the ego.

You are already the timeless; consciousness is the timeless reality; you can only be conscious in the present moment. What you think is time is a product of the mind, and that time only has reality in the present. Therefore the present is all there is. What seemingly takes time is the dissolution of the illusion and unveiling of the real. But the illusion was never real to begin with, and the real was always there, so ultimately, nothing is really being changed. It's more of a clear recognition of the illusion as an illusion rather than mistaking it as the real. From the perspective of our finite mind, the process seems to take time, so while you still believe that you are the identity, then take the time to disentangle yourself from it.

Your identity is not like a singular object that you can just easily pick out and be done with it, because it is often dispersed in various fragments. And your mental entities are alive; they can combine, disassemble, shapeshift and intertwine with one another. So if you study yourself in fragments, then you will be continuously lost in their illusions. You must see the whole, the source beneath all the masks, and to do that. You must pay absolute attention.

> "Such awareness is like living with a snake in the room; you watch its every movement, you are very, very sensitive to the slightest sound it makes. Such a state of attention is total energy; in such awareness the totality of yourself is revealed in an instant."[12] (Jiddu Krishnamurti)

Paying attention is not the same as concentration. If you are using effort to focus on a particular area, then the direction of focus will be biased and so will create conflict; focus on one area vs. another. Absolute attention has no direction; it sees the whole as it is; it's a cessation of effort, but simultaneously it requires total energy—an intensity to look. Where there's dissipation of energy, there's hidden agenda, and so the influence of attention. You cannot go around chasing your thought entities, because the one chasing the thought is the thought. And when you chase—there will be bias, so you end up looking at what is not necessary and avoiding what is necessary. Thus, the mental entities have to appear to you while you remain as the absolute awareness.

The instant your conditioned patterns touch awareness—its hold over you would dissolve. The very seeing of your conditioning would bring about instant action. When you are aware that your hand is on fire, you do not need to derive a course of action intellectually—your very awareness of the situation would instantly move your hand away from the fire.

You may notice that there are subtle tendencies where your attention seems to go toward certain thoughts while avoiding others. It is important to be aware of such tendencies. In the beginning, you can use some effort to pull your attention away from the enticing thoughts or force your attention to go toward the uncomfortable thoughts. Eventually, the attention itself would know which direction to go. Because the repressed energies are longing to be freed—they will naturally go towards awareness. Also, the enticing thoughts will lose their appeal when awareness steps out of its lure.

It takes some effort to reach the effortless state, similar to unclenching a fist, if your hand had been clenched into a fist for years, then you may need to exert some effort to relax your hand into its natural state, but once the energy is equilibrated, it takes no effort to maintain the natural state.

CHAPTER SIX: AWARENESS

DISSOLVING LAYERS OF TRAPPED EMOTIONS

The ego's core substance mostly lies in the layers upon layers of our trapped emotional pain, so even if you had come to a clear seeing of the timeless state, your pain would still cause you to have a strong pull towards unconsciousness. This is because feelings linger in the body much longer than thought. Your mind may be liberated from ego, but when your heart is not, then your energies will not naturally be pleasant. Thus, you will be compelled to seek joy elsewhere, and you will get into modes of striving over and over again.

You can dissolve your unprocessed pain by placing your attention on your inner body. When you do that, you are soaking all your emotional energies in awareness. When that happens, your pain will start to surface and process itself. This is an extremely uncomfortable thing to do for most of us because we are so used to running away from our pain. We instinctually distract ourselves with activities so that we don't have to face our pain. This is where you need to be extremely aware and see what you are doing to distract yourself and what justifications you are using for such distractions.

Many of us think that we need to fill up our time with work and activities so that we can grow and make progress in our lives, but what we are really doing is avoiding our uncomfortable feelings and memories. You need to be aware of what you are unwilling to face because whatever emotion you don't look at will perpetuate within your body. As you hold the light of awareness on your pain-body, your trapped energies will slowly bubble up layer by layer.

The feelings on the pain-body's surface layers are often easily namable, as you can identify it as jealousy, anger, hatred, anxiety, or hopelessness. As the layers get deeper and deeper, the feelings get more and more unnameable. You can perhaps only identify the feelings using qualitative descriptions, like blackness, heaviness, voltaic, stuffiness, torridness, and knottiness. In the deepest parts of the pain-body, you may no longer be able to describe the feeling at all, as they become a raw sensation. You just have to experience them as it is.

You don't need to identify your feelings, as the

identification is just a concept; when feelings are actually experienced, their qualities will change and can combine with others second by second, so it's unnecessary to put a label on it. Although you may find that some feelings do center on a distinct quality—like the explosiveness and the heatedness of anger—and sometimes it may be helpful to understand what kinds of feelings are stored within you, so that you can use your memories and imaginations to draw them out. But ultimately, it's more important to be with the feelings without mental interference, as that's how the feelings actually get processed.

When you define a feeling, you are actually separating yourself from it, as there's the you—the feeler—and then there's the feeling. This is an unconscious attempt by the ego to try to control the feeling—be conscious of this process. When you experience the feelings fully, you allow the feeling to express itself completely. Subsequently, the painful energies will dissolve into awareness. Your sustained attention on the emotional charges will equilibrate your state of consciousness.

When your consciousness becomes less polarized, it will also become more expansive, deepened, and sensitive, so you are more likely to catch yourself getting into divisive thinking patterns or unconscious behavior. Thus, your consciousness becomes more difficult to get back into a polarized state again, because polarization requires a lot of energy. When you live more consciously, your energy will come more and more to a state of unshakable serenity.

Sometimes your repressed feelings may not come up to the surface despite you having watched your emotional state for a long time. Do not get discouraged and frustrated; instead, just be patient and maintain your watchfulness. Otherwise, you will generate further negativity and further strengthen your pain-body. Be willing to watch until your last breath, even if there are no changes; don't expect to get a reward at the end. If your pain has completely dissolved, then you will be naturally watchful and pleasant. Still, sometimes there are lingering pains—like a knot in the heart—be okay with letting it stay there as long as it needs.

There will also be times where the painful feelings have come up to the surface, but they do not seem to change. When that happens, you may feel extremely uncomfortable—like you are completely drowned in excruciating pain. At those times, you may feel compelled to use a drug or do something else to get away from it as quickly as possible—again, be patient and alert; relinquish your resistance to what is. Sooner or later, the energies will start to transform, as no phenomena are static. You will feel very cathartic when the energies are released. And you will eventually learn to cherish such moments, because you get to finally expose the poisons—that were buried in your system for so long—to the light of awareness. This feeling of burning is named beautifully by Mooji as white fire, because it is the holy fire that cleanses your soul by burning away the impurities—that is, the ego.

There are instances where you can invoke the trapped feelings into the surface. If you have been carefully watching your mental state, you may notice that there are some thoughts that you tend to avoid. For example, if you had a very traumatic break-up, then whatever you come across that reminds you of your ex-partner, you start to clench up; your thoughts and feelings start to run away from the emerging pain. You may even find yourself getting disturbed by hearing words like "love, sex, girlfriend, boyfriend" in contexts that have nothing to do with your ex-partner. This is where you can summon some courage and invoke your hidden emotions by visualizing what disturbs you the most. A mind's projection can mimic an actual experience to a very high degree. That's why some scientists even go so far as to conclude that the brain can't tell the difference between imagination and reality. Even though it is ultimately untrue, but visualization can still be a powerful tool to invoke your trapped feelings.

When you visualize the worst scenario, don't be afraid to go near what surfaces, then maintain your watchfulness throughout the energy movement. You may find that there are various feelings and justifications covering up your darkest and most frightening feelings and memories. You need to be very courageous and alert in order to penetrate through all the fear to reach the core.

If you have a lot of anger charges, you can visualize a scenario where you would get extremely angry —like being insulted by someone that you vehemently hate—and then watch your anger from the beginning to the end; feel how the emotion changes in the body. And also, watch your mind; see the kind of antagonistic thoughts that gets generated; try to remain as awareness instead of being completely lost in the thoughts or emotions.

If you have a lot of jealousy, you can visualize your partner or ex-partner cheating on you, then watch the fury that arises to cover up your jealousy. Do not get carried away with the rage or run to hateful thoughts. Instead go further into the underlying blackness and sourness that comes from the jealousy. Do not distract yourself with entertainment or escape to pleasant thoughts; go further into the dreadfulness without losing consciousness.

If you have a lot of fear, you can visualize what you are most afraid of—like losing your loved ones— and watch how your body trembles and how the hopelessness is engulfing you. When you fully go into your pain, you will eventually come to a stillness. Your emotional response from subsequent visualizations will become less and less potent.

When you practice watchfulness either during visualizations or in solitude, you will be much more capable of being watchful in actual challenging situations. You will find yourself being aware of your anger earlier and earlier during your emotional outburst. One day you are completely aware of how you are triggered, and at that point, you will feel like you have a choice in how to respond. Eventually, you will find that you are no longer emotional invested in the situations where you would normally explode; you naturally choose to remain un-reactive.

In the beginning stages of your practice, your awareness is one with the emotion, so you are completely unconscious and have become anger. There's no internal conflict as you feel completely justified in your actions, and you may feel quite good about it. However, you are unknowingly poisoning yourself and others. People do the stupidest things when they are angry; you yourself know that you never like to be on the receiving end of someone else's outburst. In the middle stages, your awareness separates from the anger, so there's the you in anger, then there's another you that is watching the anger, and that you could get judgemental, so you need to be very alert on that as well. Do not add further conflict by judging or suppressing your anger, but if you catch yourself doing so then just watch that.

Toward the latter stages, your awareness is one with itself, so it's no longer mixed up with other negativities. However, when this happens, it does not mean that you no longer need to be watchful, because you think you are more "enlightened" than everybody else and are always justified in your behaviors. You still need to conduct yourself consciously. The only difference in the latter stages is you will find that it's effortless to be watchful.

> "Sustained conscious attention severs the link between the pain-body and your thought processes and brings about the process of transmutation. It is as if the pain becomes fuel for the flame of your consciousness, which then burns more brightly as a result. This is the esoteric meaning of the ancient art of alchemy. The transmutation of base metal into gold, of suffering into consciousness. The split within is healed, and you become whole again."[1] (Eckhart Tolle, *The Power of Now*)

Here's a first-person account of the process of self-inquiry: when I was young, I experienced repeated forms of mistreatment like being disrespected, being ignored, and so on, so I developed strong feelings of unworthiness. I am afraid of this feeling; I don't want to feel like that, and I don't want others to treat me like that, so I try not to be like that. I create an image of myself being worthy, and

I escape to that image. I will do whatever I can to make sure that others see me as this image.

When I talk to others, I subtly mention the important people I know and the things I've accomplished in the hopes of other people acknowledging me as someone important. When I socialize like that, I'm not genuinely interested in other people, as I'm more concerned about my own image. When I'm in my head and not in reality, I am not in sync with the social environment, and so my conversations do not vibe well with others, and people tend to ignore me as a result. Whenever others don't treat me the way I want to be treated, I get deeply disturbed; I freeze; I close up to shield myself from my unworthiness. I may try to ignore social situations in the future in order to avoid going through such experiences again.

I will also try harder to win other's approval, so I construct another image of me as a humble person, because I got good treatment when I acted humbly in certain situations. And now, my image as a humble person conflict with my image as a superior person, so in every social situation, I'm confused between my multiple personalities. Also, even when I did win everyone's approval, my painful feelings are still there, so I need to constantly seek other's approval.

I see that all of my problems essentially stem from my feelings of unworthiness. I see what I am—unworthy—as a fact, and what I want to be—worthy —is an idea, so I stand by the fact and not the idea. And because I clearly see that it is there, I cannot do anything about it; I cannot escape, repress, or judge it. I see that all such efforts are futile because I cannot get rid of it, so I must look at it and accept it; I cease all effort and resistance to it. And once the feeling is fully accepted without even the agenda to accept it, the feeling loses its abstraction. The feeling has come so close to me that I can no longer name it. I no longer know what it is. I am simply experiencing it as is. The feeling then transforms into awareness; my energy is no longer polarized in multiple directions. Such energy has fragrances of joy and love.

When I stop comparing myself to anybody else, then all of my unworthiness goes. I am what I am; I see with absolute conviction that I cannot be anything else. Subsequently, I no longer need to mentally figure out what to do and what to say all the time, because my natural state is by default in tune with life. The personal "I" no longer does anything. Instead, all actions come from the universal "I," and the universal "I" can naturally socialize.

The universal "I" is not identified with anything. I am neither man nor woman, neither introvert nor extrovert. I will only be what is needed in the situation given. When I need to be assertive, I will be, and when I need to be yielding, I will also. And so, my response will be spontaneous, intelligent, and sane. I acknowledge my role for practical purposes only; when somebody calls my name, I will answer, and when somebody demands the services of my job, I will fulfill their request, but I no longer derive my sense of self from my roles. I no longer seek to expand my sense of self through any of my activities. Therefore all selfishness is gone. Only activities that do not come from the need to be selfless can really be selfless.

THE NATURE OF AWARENESS

One of the first realizations that you may come across while performing your self-inquiry is that you are not your thoughts, because you know that you can observe them. Thoughts are coming and going, but you are not coming and going. You are that in which the thought phenomena appear. Although the voice in your head feels like your voice, but the sense that this is my voice can also be observed. Therefore, the "thinker"—that you think is you—is actually the thought. The "thinker" is not separate from the thought as if it's elsewhere doing the thinking; that "thinker" is just an imagination.

What is behind the thoughts is the unconditioned observer, and this observer cannot influence thought in any way. Because any influence of thought will be part of thought, and so is no longer the observer. This observer is not what you think it is, because whatever it is that you can think about is in itself a thought. The unconditioned observer cannot be touched by thought. So how can we know this observer?

Can the observer itself be observed? The observer can observe thoughts, feelings, and pretty much any knowable experience, but it can never observe itself. A knife can cut any object, but can it cut itself? Your eyes can look at anything, but can it look at itself directly? And I don't mean through a mirror, since a mirror image is only a reflection of the eye. So for the act of observing to exist, a subject-object relationship must exist between the observer and what is observed, meaning that the observer must be fundamentally different or separate from what is observed to bring about the act of observing.

You are aware when your attention moves its concentration from one area to another and when it expands or contracts. Therefore, you are not the movement of attention. You are aware of the changes in your moods, sensations, and feelings. You know the state of your memory—sometimes your memories are fuzzy, and at other times they are clear—so you are beyond all psychological phenomena. You know the passage of time, the qualities of space, and the presence and absence of consciousness—when you're in deep sleep, there is no time and space, and when you wake up, suddenly they appeared. Thus, you are beyond all dimensions, all universal laws. Although this has always been the case, you can be more conscious of it.

"Everything you can perceive comes and goes, including your own body. You are the one looking at time, objects, and even thoughts and emotions. Through the senses, you are able to observe everything that is perceived as life, as manifestation, as existence. And behind the eyes – in the realm of thought, emotion, and memory – these are perceived with the eyes of inner perception. Your sense of being a particular person is also perceived.

Regardless of whether the object of perception is physical and can thus be measured for colour, shape, and size, or whether what is being perceived is something more subtle like thought, feeling, and sensation, all are phenomena. It is the sense of 'I' that perceives them. First 'I' must be there …"[2] (Mooji, *Vaster Than Sky, Greater Than Space*)

Once you know what you are not—which is all that is phenomenal—you must continue to investigate what you are. Now, the question comes, what is this "observer"? This question must interest you because this "observer" is not only mysterious but also very obvious, since it has always been with you. However, it also eludes you in the sense that it itself cannot be directly observed—it can only do the observing. It is important that you remain as this "observer" experientially, try to get to know it, not mentally, like upholding a visual image of a blank space, or concluding it like it is something produced by the brain. Instead, simply remain knowingly as the observer of your experience, and feel its qualities. Similar to knowing the sun, you cannot directly look at it, but you can use your peripheral vision to see its light, and you can also use your senses to feel its warmth.

Everything that you have experienced in your life, you know that you are aware of them, correct? Everything that was, that is, and that ever will be must occur within your awareness, meaning that awareness must be there first before anything else becomes knowable. The common element in all experience is that you know them.

Remember yourself at any age, has the way in which you know your experience changed? What has changed was the content of awareness, but awareness itself is always the same. This is why people have the feeling that they haven't aged, even though they can clearly see that their bodies have aged. We have this deep intuition because our essence is awareness, and awareness never changes. It is always in the most pristine state. Children are more in touch with this intuition because they haven't been conditioned as much yet. This is why many children have no fear of death; they are not unconcerned about death because they are just so young, but because they are more one with the eternal.

When you become aware of this dimensionless state within you, you can start to see that no matter how many places you have been to physically or mentally, but there is a part of you that has never moved. No matter how many words you have spoken—there is a part of you that is always silent. And no matter how many changes you have been through—there is a part of you that has never become anything. You can rationalize this in the thinking mind by saying that, of course, no matter where you are, you are always here and now. Still, beyond the thinking mind, you can really feel this reality.

Awareness is the void-like presence that is in the background of every experience. You may find a lot of resistance to it because the ego does not like the emptiness; it wants to feel like it has become something and that all its past accomplishments were not for nothing; without its history, it loses its existence. If you go into the void that you have feared all your life and tried to run from by filling it up with endless "things," then you will find infinity itself.

Awareness is space-like and always still, eternal and ever-present. It's everywhere and nowhere simultaneously. Its nature is peaceful and loving, yielding and transparent. Awareness is so pure that it does not even know that it's pure. Awareness is the formless; therefore, it can experience the form. It is the infinite; therefore it can experience the finite. It is the timeless; therefore, it can experience the ephemeral. Thus, you—the awareness—cannot die; everything in this life can come and go, but you cannot come and go. You cannot be touched by anything; even the most traumatic experience cannot affect you. What can you do to disturb space? To damage space? Space is imperturbable and indestructible.

Your mind may think that the ending of the body will bring an end to awareness. The ending of the body will not bring an end to awareness, only the mind will stop, and it will mistake its own ending with the ending of awareness. When consciousness goes, that can also be witnessed. You can also start to see that you don't even have a choice in the witnessing. The witnessing just goes on and on. Whatever choice there is is part of the phenomena that is being witnessed but not the witness itself. Everything is just a passing show; bodies, worlds come and go; you are just watching.

"For the soul there is never birth nor death. Nor, having once been, does he ever cease to be. He is unborn, eternal, ever-existing, undying and primeval. He is not slain when the body is slain."[3] (*Bhagavad Gita*)

> "The human brain is a highly differentiated form through which consciousness enters this dimension. It contains approximately one

hundred billion nerve cells (called neurons), about the same number as there are stars in our galaxy, which could be seen as a macrocosmic brain. The brain does not create consciousness, but consciousness created the brain, the most complex physical form on earth, for its expression. When the brain gets damaged, it does not mean you lose consciousness. It means consciousness can no longer use that form to enter this dimension. You cannot lose consciousness because it is, in essence, who you are. You can only lose something that you have, but you cannot lose something that you are."[4] (Eckhart Tolle, *A New Earth*)

CHAPTER SEVEN: REALITY

THE NATURE
OF EXISTENCE

For many people, despite having clearly seen that what they essentially are is not the body, they will still reject that understanding because the model of reality provided by science or religion are so prevalent in society and have seeped deeply into the collective psyche. Many people will choose to deny their experiential evidence of reality as not to seem crazy to others or themselves.

The widely accepted scientific model of reality is that some phenomena called the big bang occurred. Suddenly, this universe came into existence. And through the interactions of various elements, intelligent organisms like human beings are formed, inside of which exists a brain that can produce consciousness that allows us to experience the world. This model separates the universe into what is objective and subjective. Thus, there is an objective world that is made up of matter, and then there is a subjective experience of that world that is made up of mind. In this model, matter takes precedence because, without matter, there would be no consciousness. The subjective experience is irrelevant compared to the objective reality, as the universe will carry on without consciousness. This model considers the universe to be more of a random accident and so is inherently meaningless. As Friedrich Nietzsche famously declared: "God is Dead." This model also considers the world to be fundamentally chaotic, and so it needs to be brought into order by the "intelligent" beings in the universe.

The problem with the scientific model is that we can never prove the existence of an objective world; all objectivity appears to us in subjectivity. There needs to be a knower for there to be the known. We cannot separate ourselves from the world as if what we see "out there" is independent of us. Does sound exist if there is no ear to hear it? Does light exist if there is nothing to reflect it? If there is only vacuum and no surface to stop light, then the stream of light would just flow endlessly in an infinite vacuum; thus, there would be no light. Without the experiencer, there would be no experience. The world is vastly different for a human being compared to another organism. What we see as light and daytime, a nocturnal animal will see as darkness and nighttime, so which perspective is correct?

Before science, people have explained the nature of the world through the teachings of various religions. Their explanation is that God—the creator —created everything according to his will. People have accepted this conclusion because they can see vast intelligence everywhere, from a cell to a human body. In this model, the universe is not just a senseless accident. Instead, it has meaning, and each individual has a purpose.

The problem with the religious model is that once God has become an idea, a form, then we have separated ourselves from God. If we are different from God, then our agenda must also differ from God's. We are fundamentally imperfect and sinful, while God is all-powerful and perfect. Thus we spend our entire life trying to meet the expectations of God so we could live a "purposeful" life and go to heaven. Also, the agenda of God will always be made up from our minds, so they will differ from religion to religion. Hence, we will not only have conflict between ourselves and God but also between God and God. When we see others worshipping a different God from us, we call them a heretic. Once God has taken the form of a creator, there will inevitably be contradictions because if there is a creator, then who or what created the creator? And if God is all-powerful and good, then why does he allow evil and suffering in the world?

Neither the scientific model nor the religious model is inherently wrong. However, they are both limited because it is only a conceptual model of reality. When people have accepted either model as the truth, they will go through their entire life with the understanding that they are fragile existence and will eventually come to an end. Naturally, they will live in constant fear and be compelled to follow various authorities to protect their existence. As long as the model of reality is rooted in concepts, the truth will be partial—which will lead to contradictions. This is why even within science or religion, there are different conflicting models.

"The clash between science and religion has not shown that religion is false and science is true. It has shown that all systems of definition are relative to various purposes, and that none of them actually 'grasp' reality."[1] (Alan Watts)

No model of reality can substitute reality itself; the most solid evidence you have of reality is that you are aware that experiencing is taking place. Everything else can be false, but this is the one thing you can be sure of; you cannot prove that you are not conscious. Even if reality is a simulation, awareness still needs to be there for experience to happen. "The only truth is I AM – I Exist. That is the only truth. Everything else is a concept."[2] (Ramesh Balsekar)

The more you sink your attention back to its source, the more you will bring the background of experience into the foreground. When you realize that the source of all experience is awareness, you may no longer be swayed by external events because your essence will disidentify itself from the world of form. Subsequently, your fear of death will go. However, this is only the half stage of realization because there is still a layer of suffering that many of us may have. We would then question why we are stuck as the witness to this particular life, and even though the body is not me, I still have to endure the suffering. This is when the ego has identified itself as awareness, as if the awareness is an object. When awareness becomes an object, then it becomes a helpless witness that is completely detached from life. Many people can get stuck at this stage of realization, and they would find life to be completely meaningless. They would often question their purpose in existence.

THE COLLAPSE
OF DUALITY

We need to first separate awareness and experience so we can recognize the source and substance of all experience. But, to realize the whole truth, we need to collapse awareness and experience. The observer must go with the observed; they are the two sides of the same coin, so what is observed is actually the observer itself, as Jiddu Krishnamurti stated: "the observer is the observed." You are simultaneously one with the world and also beyond it. "All there is, is Consciousness." (Ramesh Balsekar)

We cannot know awareness as any kind of object because it is the pure subject that is beyond even the concept of object and subject. Suppose we conceive the subject as an idea, in that case, that idea is also knowable, meaning that it will also become an object. There's no experiencer nor the experienced. There is just the experiencing.

Many teachers need to use positive attributes to describe awareness like love, happiness, infinite, and so on, as a way to communicate the inherent qualities of awareness. However, awareness cannot really be described by any concept. The love that comes from awareness is beyond love and hate; awareness is the greater good that includes both positives and negatives. Life is both living and dying; it's a single process, only our mind has divided it into two. Would you say that you are living or dying? Our body is deteriorating and going towards the grave every second, but we are also alive. We need to use concepts like life and death to contrast the different aspects of life for communication purposes, but they are all describing the same reality. Concepts have relevance psychologically but not existentially; in reality, there is no duality.

So, do not get stuck on concepts and think that once you realize awareness, you will be happy all the time. No one can be happy all the time. Happiness as a state will invariably change. Awareness is the background of all changeful states. Nevertheless, once you are more aligned with awareness, the suffering caused by changeful states like pleasure-and-pain, gain-and-loss will lose its grip on you, so you will more effortlessly remain in a happy state. Realizing awareness also does not mean that you as the person will become infinite and eternal, the mind will always be finite, and the body will always be ephemeral; they need to be that way so awareness can experience different bodies and different worlds, but awareness itself is not bound by space and time.

> "After people die, other people are born, and they're all you. It's just that you can only experience one life at a time. Wherever beings exist throughout all the galaxies, you are all of them—when they come into being, that's *you* coming into being. You don't remember the past in the same way that you don't have to think about how to make your thyroid work. You don't have to know how to shine the sun, you just do it, just as you breathe without thinking about it."[3] (Alan Watts, *Out of Your Mind*)

> "Awareness is primordial; it is the original state, beginningless, endless, uncaused, unsupported, without parts, without change. Consciousness is on contact, a reflection against a surface, a state of duality. There can be no consciousness without awareness, but there can be awareness without consciousness, as in deep sleep. Awareness is absolute, consciousness is relative to its content; consciousness is always of something. Consciousness is partial and changeful, awareness is total, changeless... And it is the common matrix of every experience."[4] (Nisargadatta Maharaj, *I Am That*)

Do not be confused by the words. Consciousness and awareness can be used interchangeably—as often done so by many teachers. This book does so as well. Maharaj has differentiated the two to explain the absolute; when he says consciousness, he refers to the personal consciousness, while he uses Awareness to refer to the universal Consciousness. Maharaj is trying to say that even in the absence of personal consciousness, as in deep sleep, there is still the absolute. When you are in deep sleep, consciousness is not attending to anything, so it's in its purest state. When you are the infinite, no finite object can be in your experience. Otherwise, the infinite would no longer be the infinite. You are beyond the presence and absence of personal consciousness because you know both states, the person is gone in deep sleep, but you are not.

The more you see that your essence is awareness, the more you will feel the unity of all forms. Because if awareness has no qualities within you, then it must not have any qualities in any other form. Whatever quality there is, is part of the ephemeral world, and so is not your timeless essence. Therefore your essence is not different from any other sentient life. It is the same quality-less awareness that is experiencing existence in all forms.

This quality-less awareness cannot be separated because it is kind of like space, and can space be divided? What is the number of spaces in this world? If we enclose a space by constructing a building, is the space within the enclosure different from the space outside it? Can any form separate space? Space permeates all forms. Without space, there would be no form; without silence, there would be no sound. As written in *The Heart Sutra*: "Form is emptiness and emptiness is form."

> "Just as the difference between the space in a pot and the space outside it disappears when the pot is demolished, so also does duality disappear when it is realized that the difference between the individual consciousness and the Universal Consciousness does not in fact exist." (Ramesh Balsekar)

This space-like awareness is what religious and spiritual teachings really mean when they say God —prior to interpretation and institutionalization of the teachings. God has no form, either physically like an organism or psychologically like an idea, and everything in existence is made up of that same God. The teachings have used various words to call it, like Soul, Being, Atman, Tao, Noumena, Cosmic Law, and Source.

Many scientists have realized that theories can never arrive at the nature of existence, because conceptual knowledge can only dissect and so cannot unify. Once they know that they don't know and have abandoned their thinking mind, then awareness emerges, and the whole is seen. Some scientists have recognized the nature of existence, and they have called it: energy ($E = MC^2$) or the

Divine Matrix.

> "As the big bang's explosive force ripped into the emptiness of the existing void, it carried with it more than just the heat and light that we'd expect. It also burst forth as a pattern of energy that became the blueprint for all that is now and all that can ever be. ... It is this net or web of energy that continues to expand throughout the cosmos as the quantum essence of all things, including us and our surroundings. This is the energy that connects our lives as the Divine Matrix. ...
>
> How can we be so sure that everything in the universe is really connected? To answer this question, let's go back to the big bang and the University of Geneva experiment... As different as they appear from one another, there's a subtle similarity: In each, the connection that's being explored exists between two things that were once physically joined. In the case of the experiment, splitting a single photon into two identical particles created the twins, and this was done to assure that both were alike in every way. The fact that the photons and the particles from the big bang were once physically part of one another is the key to their connectivity. It appears that once something is joined, it is always connected, whether it remains physically linked or not. ... There's every reason to believe that the entangled state that

links particles that are separated today also applies to the stuff of our universe that was connected before the big bang. Technically, everything that was merged within our pea-sized cosmos 13 to 20 billion years ago is still connected! And the energy that does the connecting is what Planck described as the 'matrix' of everything."[5] (Gregg Braden, *The Divine Matrix*)

On the microscopic level, we can see that complex organisms like human beings are really composed of simpler biological building blocks that appear to have a will of their own, but when seen as a whole, they form a singular entity. Similarly, on a macroscopic level, human beings and everything else in the universe appears to have their own will. However, together they form the whole of existence with a singular will. On the surface of the ocean, each individual wave looks like a separate wave, but they are made up of the same ocean. We, on the surface—with our body and mind—look as if we are separate, but we are really expressions of the same Awareness.

You may clearly think that you are separate because as sure as you are of being conscious, you are also sure of what's outside you and what's within you. Typically, we have divided our experience into two aspects: the internal and the external. Our external experiences are perceived through the senses, while our internal world is made up of our psychological processes. And this line between the external and the internal—we are completely sure about. But if we take a closer look at this, is there really such a line?

On the one hand, we can say that all is external because we cannot really control anything. Do you see that there is always a discrepancy between what you want to do and what you actually do? Your thoughts, emotions, and behavior don't always align with your conscious intent, so your body and mind are kind of like a machine that you own rather than something that you are. You can see that everything you experience is really just a happening—your breath is happening just as the sun is illuminating. The key is that you are the one that is seeing everything, so what you can see cannot be you. I don't mean seeing like a physical seeing; it's more of an aware seeing. You are aware of the perceptions of your eye just as you are aware of the thoughts in your mind.

How many times in life did you not want what you got, but only to realize a few years later that was exactly what you needed at the time? And how many times you got exactly what you wanted only to realize that wasn't what you wanted at all? The intelligence that seems to operate beyond your will is far greater than your own mind. When you give an infant food, the infant will not try to put it in their nose or ears before putting it in their mouth. The infant instinctively knows what to do because it is really the greater intelligence at work, and this intelligence is not only responsible for turning food into a brain, but it is also responsible for every single movement in the universe. If this intelligence is allowed its full expression without being stifled by the ego, then the right thoughts, actions, and life conditions will come on their own.

To avoid confusion here, the ego is also manufactured by the same intelligence as an obstacle to challenge itself; the ego does not really exist. On the absolute level, there's no such thing as the right action as all actions are performed by the same intelligence. But on the relative level—when you think you have a will—then the ego is problematic.

From the other perspective, we can also say that all existence is internal because everything must appear within our consciousness for them to have any existential value. So we are really responsible for all the workings of the universe, including the illumination of the sun. As Jesus said: "the kingdom of God is within you."⁶ Therefore, the line between what is you and not you is really arbitrary. "What we call 'I' is just a swinging door which moves when we inhale and when we exhale."⁷ (Shunryu Suzuki)

> "What you see out here is a neurological experience. ... You may feel therefore that the ex-

ternal world is all inside my skull. You've got to correct that, with the thought that your skull is also in the external world. So you suddenly begin to feel 'Wow, what kind of situation is this? It's inside me, and I'm inside it, and it's inside me, and I'm inside it.' But that's the way it is.

This is the what you could call transaction, rather than interaction between the individual and the world. Just like, for example, in buying and selling. There cannot be an act of buying unless there is simultaneously an act of selling, and vice versa. So the relationship between the environment and the organism is transactional. The environment grows the organism, and in turn the organism creates the environment. The organism turns the sun into light, but it requires there be an environment containing a sun for there to be an organism at all. And the answer to it simply is they're all one process. It isn't that organisms by chance came into the world. This world is the sort of environment which grows organisms."[8] (Alan Watts)

Many spiritual seekers seek an enlightenment experience in which they can merge with the divine so that the line between the internal and the external can be shattered. But such an experience can never come because the line was never there in the first place. As Nisargadatta Maharaj explained in *I*

Am That:

"Your expectation of something unique and dramatic, of some wonderful explosion, is merely hindering and delaying your Self Realization. You are not to expect an explosion, for the explosion has already happened... There is only one mistake you are making: you take the inner for the outer and the outer for the inner. ... The mind and feelings are external, but you take them to be intimate. You believe the world to be objective, while it is entirely a projection of your psyche. That is the basic confusion and no new explosion will set it right!"[9]

GOD'S GAME

We can understand the world through an analogy; if you look at your dreams, within the dream world, you have always taken the form of a dream character—doesn't matter what it is—it may be your waking state body, an alien creature, or an invisible witness. But you must be a finite object within that dream to experience the dream world. Otherwise, there would be no dream. And what is that dream world made up of? It is all made up of the same substance as the dream character, which is your mind, which is you.

What happens in the dream cannot affect you —the dreamer—whether your dream character knows that it is dreaming or not. So in the dream, you are both the creator and the creation, while you are also beyond it. Similarly, in the waking state, the seeming separation between you —the subject—and the objects of experience are also illusory as they are both one and the same. As Nisargadatta Maharaj put it: "The world you perceive is made of consciousness; what you call matter is consciousness itself." This is why there are supernatural phenomena because everything is intrinsically linked; all is one. There's no you and God; there is only God. There is only you. "The eye with which I see God is the same eye with which God sees me." (Meister Eckhart)

God cannot know anything because God already is everything—like water not being able to know water. God needed to split herself so that her limited form could experience herself as something other than herself, but in actuality, what she is really experiencing is only herself.

Existence needs separation to allow the play of life to happen. We can observe that all phenomena exist in duality, like cause/effect, male/female, chaos/order, subject/object, good/evil, and so on. Life appears to us as if they are different things, but this is only due to our limited mind being able to perceive one aspect of duality at a time. If I can see black, then I cannot see white, so the mind came to the conclusion that they are separate, but in actuality, they are one thing. This is the fundamental truth illustrated by the yin yang symbol. Yin is not separate from yang; they give existence to each other. Without yang, there would be no yin. If there is only black, then we will not know black because we have nothing to contrast it with; white is black; yin is yang. As God explained to Neale Donald Walsch in *Conversations with God*:

> "The one thing that All That Is knew is that there was nothing else. And so It could, and

would, never know Itself from a reference point outside of Itself. Such a point did not exist. Only one reference point existed, and that was the single place within. The 'Is-Not Is.' The Am-Not Am.

Still, the All of Everything chose to know Itself experientially.

This energy—this pure, unseen, unheard, un-observed, and therefore unknown-by-anyone-else energy—chose to experience Itself as the utter magnificence It was. In order to do this, It realized It would have to use a reference point within.

It reasoned, quite correctly, that any portion of Itself would necessarily have to be less than the whole, and that if It thus simply divided It-self into portions, each portion, being less than the whole, could look back on the rest of Itself and see magnificence.

And so All That Is divided Itself—becoming, in one glorious moment, that which is this, and that which is that. For the first time, this and that existed, quite apart from each other. And still, both existed simultaneously. As did all that was neither.

Thus, three elements suddenly existed: that which is here. That which is there. And that which is neither here nor there—but which must exist for here and there to exist.

It is the nothing which holds the everything. It is the non-space which holds the space. It is the all which holds the parts."[10]

"The Tao gives birth to One. One gives birth to Two. Two gives birth to Three. Three gives birth to all things."[11] (Lao Tzu, *Tao Te Ching*)

You may wonder, why is it that we do not live as we are God? Since most people fear and suffer throughout their entire life. Well, no single answer is correct because we are all God, so any opinion is equally valid. One explanation is that God intentionally forgets his true identity in the world of form, so that he can experience the thrills of the world as if it's a real threat to him. Similar to when you fall asleep, you forget that you are the dreamer, so that you can experience the dream world as if it's real.

You may also question why does God allow despicable acts of evil like violence toward children? Yes, injustice, violence, and suffering are a fact; we cannot deny that. But there is no sufferer, because God is both the perpetrator and the victim; it is God acting onto God. This is all just an act, a play. "Remember ... that in almost all the stories you enjoy there have to be bad people as well as good people, for the thrill of the tale is to find out how the good people will get the better of the bad"[12] (Alan Watts). From one perspective, life is really just a game of hide and seek that God is playing with himself. As Alan Watts explained in *The Book on the Taboo Against Knowing Who You Are*:

> "God ... likes to play hide-and-seek, but because there is nothing outside God, he has no one but himself to play with. But he gets over this difficulty by pretending that he is not himself. ... He pretends that he is you and I and all the people in the world, all the animals, all the plants... In this way he has strange and wonderful adventures, some of which are terrible and frightening. But these are just like bad dreams, for when he wakes up they will disappear.
>
> Now when God plays hide and pretends that he is you and I, he does it so well that it takes him a long time to remember where and how he hid himself. But that's the whole fun of it— just what he wanted to do. He doesn't want to find himself too quickly, for that would spoil the game. ..."[12]

THE ABSOLUTE VIEW

Language is rooted in duality, as every word must have its own opposite, otherwise it cannot exist. If I say consciousness is the source of all phenomena or that you are not the phenomena, then I have separated consciousness from phenomena as if there is consciousness and then there are phenomena. This is not true because they are not separate; just as the screen is not separate from the movie, there is only the screen, there is only consciousness. However, if I say that there is only consciousness, then simultaneously, I am also implying that there is something other than consciousness because otherwise, why even make that statement in the first place? What is the absolute cannot be said. This is why many teachers say that the highest teaching is silence. "Those who know don't talk. Those who talk don't know"[13] (Lao Tzu). Consciousness does not speak; the person speaks. Consciousness is.

Therefore, if we are to talk about reality, then

we must dip into duality. The consciousness-only model of reality is as follows: Consciousness is the single dreamer, dreaming up infinite dreams. Each dream is what we are experiencing from our particular perspective. Free will is an illusion because there are no individuals to have free will. Your will is God's will. "Not an atom moves except by His Will" (Ramana Maharshi). Whatever thought you had and will have is God's thought. Even if you reject this notion, it is not you who is rejecting it. It is God who is rejecting it. "Events happen, deeds are done, but there is no individual doer thereof." (The Buddha)

You think that you are living your life, but life is actually living you. Life is the doer, and you—as your body and mind—are the deed. Every perception, thought, feeling, sensation, action, and movement of attention are all part of the passing show. Your true self as awareness is only watching all that; you have no control because the controller is part of the creation. Like a dream, the dream character is part of the dream world. Thus, whatever action it thinks it's doing is illusory, as it is really done by the dreamer. The dreamer cannot partake in the dream, because it will be part of the dream and thus is no longer the dreamer.

The universal consciousness is the true orchestrator of life. Still, it needs to localize itself into a personal consciousness in order to experience its own creation. Only the personal consciousness can experience anything phenomenal, and to the personal consciousness, everything is pre-determined. However, the personal consciousness is a microcosm of the universal consciousness. So people will feel like they have some control over their life—as it is part of the dream experience—but ultimately, that control is an illusion. Some physicists have already arrived at this conclusion. At the end of Stephen Hawking's essay *Is Everything Determined*, he concluded that it was a yes to his essay's title.

> "Everything is predetermined. Right from the time of conception, whether the conception is aborted or a baby is born – till it dies, everything is predetermined.
>
> Life is like a movie that is already in the can. We see the movie scene by scene, but the end of the movie has already been predetermined.
>
> … We think A leads to B, B leads to C, C leads to D and so on. But the arrow of destiny is double-pointed. For D to happen, C had to happen; for C to happen, B had to happen… Though everything is predetermined, knowing that will not help you in any way, as you will never know what it is that is predetermined."[14] (*Pointers from Ramesh Balsekar*)

"Whatever is destined not to happen will not happen, try as you may. Whatever is destined to happen will happen, do what you may to prevent it.

This is certain. The best course, therefore, is to remain silent." (Ramana Maharshi)

Whether something is good or bad is all made up by the mind, because we can never know how things will turn out; what seems to be a bad thing at one time may turn out a good thing at another. No event is isolated; all events are interconnected. "Whatever happened, happened for the good. Whatever is happening, is happening for the good. Whatever will happen, will also happen for the good." (*Bhagavad Gita*)

When you are judging things, your mind need to cut up the indivisible reality into pieces—which leads to distortion. Thus, to label something as good or bad is ultimately pointless, as events are as they are. From the absolute perspective, the world cannot really get anywhere, because fundamentally, it is always an expression of the same consciousness. On a relative level, things may seem to get better or worse, but all such progression is ultimately illusory.

> "How long have the planets been circling the sun? Are they getting anywhere, and do they go faster and faster in order to arrive? How often has the spring returned to the earth? Does it come faster and fancier every year, to be sure to be better than last spring, and to hurry on its way to the spring that shall outspring all springs?"[15] (Alan Watts, *The Wisdom*

of Insecurity)

The drama of the world is a show by God. Consciousness is ruining the world through some mind-body organisms, while consciousness is also fixing the world through other mind-body organisms. The conflict between the two forces is just a form of play. Neither side has the power to overcome the other because both sides are played by the same actor. This is why you can never really outwit the universe, because the universe is you.

Some people who read books like this will undergo change, while others will not. Some authors will write books like this, while others will oppose this kind of view. And all of it is part of the perfect unfolding of consciousness. Books like this intend to simply share a view in which the author knows that is ultimately untrue. The author's intention is not to cause change because he knows that it's impossible, although the author may say otherwise. The true purpose of writing books is just to write. The author can never know the outcome; this book may impact a lot of people, or it may not, but whatever happens, is beyond the individual will; it is all up to the universal will. "You have a right to perform your prescribed duties, but you are not entitled to the fruits of your actions. Never consider yourself to be the cause of the results of your activities, nor be attached to inaction."[16] (*Bhagavad Gita*)

You may carry on with your divisiveness and continue to pollute the world with your negativity. That will all be part of the perfect unfolding of life. You may resist life with all your energy and get judgemental all the time, but it will all be accepted by consciousness. What can space do to the phenomenal world? Space yields without exception and without the agenda to yield. Its nature is yielding and accepting.

Consciousness' nature is peace and joy, you may think that joy is a fleeting state, but that is only because you see it from the ego's perspective. Sounds may seem to replace silence, but silence is always there; when the ego is quiet, happiness is the default state. Awareness is self-knowing, just like the sun is self-illuminating, even if a thought has deluded the mind, but consciousness cannot be deluded. You may live in time your entire life, but it will still take place in the timeless moment; the present is the only reality. Nothing you do can ever be out of place. To think whether you should act from awareness or from the ego is actually pointless. Only the ego thinks it needs to decide. Awareness does not need to decide. Every moment is as it should be. Otherwise, it would not have happened. Does a tree need to decide where to grow its next branch? "Nothing real can be threatened. Nothing unreal exists. Herein lies the peace of God."[17] (*A Course in Miracles*)

"In spiritual circles there is great value placed on personal growth, personal improvement, becoming a better person, becoming more aware, teaching others how to become better, making the world a better and more enlightened place. The hope for a better future, the belief in an upward spiritual evolution that carries the whole race with it, is like the belief that there is something wrong and something that needs to be done. It seems hard-wired into the human mechanism but is in fact the device by which the 'divine hypnosis' operates, keeping the dream characters motivated and occupied in the dream. This belief is an illusion, and it is what creates suffering.

In Truth, in the Absolute, in All That Is, there is no evolution, no progress, no becoming better, no becoming. All is as it is. The idea that the world is in bad shape and that the present point in history is pivotal and that something has to be done, is as old as the human mind; it has always seemed thus, at every point in 'human history.' In truth everything is in perfect balance; the world never gets better and never gets worse, although to the apparent individual instruments it may seem that it does."[18] (David Carse, *Perfect Brilliant Stillness*)

Be careful of getting too attached to the absolute view because a view will always be in the realm of the relative, even if it is the truth. You as a dream character can only exist in the relative, and the dream character cannot make any absolute statements about reality. The true absolute is beyond the dream and thus cannot be grasped by the limited mind. A common pitfall for many on the spiritual path is that they become too fixated on the absolute view and thus have made it into a philosophy. Therefore, even if you know that everything is predetermined and you can do no wrong, but you are still responsible for your actions, you cannot use the absolute philosophy to justify your divisiveness.

> "This is one of the dangers of awakening: the tendency to grasp at a lopsided view. We grasp at the absolute view of awakening, and we deny anything else. It is actually the ego that fixates on the world absolute in this way, using it as an excuse for dismissing unenlightened behavior, thought patterns, and divided emotional states. As soon as we grasp at any view, we have gone blind to everything else.
>
> ... That's why so many truly enlightened beings—those who have proclaimed that everything is good, that all is well, who perceive no need to change anything or anybody —are often the very ones tending to those who are suffering, those who don't perceive truth. The truly enlightened beings are often those who dedicate their lives completely to the wel-

fare of others.

Now, why would they do that? If everything is perfect as it is, if nothing needs to change, if everything is holy and divine exactly as it is, if all is well even when all isn't well, then why would these enlightened beings dedicate their lives to the welfare of others—what would be the point? Well, there wouldn't be one. If the absolute view were the only view, they wouldn't be doing it. I would suggest that the reason so many people who get that far in their own awakening end up dedicating themselves to the welfare of others is that they haven't fixated on the absolute view. Without denying the absolute view of perfection, they are open to perceiving something more. They are open to perceiving the inherent compassion of reality itself."[19] (Adyashanti, *The End of Your World*)

From the absolute perspective, everything is perfect as it is, and you are beyond all. But from the relative perspective, there are problems and suffering everywhere, and so you need to take care of your life—even if it's just a game. Both perspectives are in the realm of duality. The true absolute is not getting attached to either perspective. You have nowhere to stand, neither in the relative nor in the absolute; you are neither the person nor God. That's why Ram Dass said: "there's nowhere where you are not, and there's nowhere where you are."

CHAPTER EIGHT: APOTHEOSIS

ENLIGHTENMENT

Enlightenment is simply the recognition of your true essence as awareness; it is not something that you become, because the fictional self cannot become anything. The one that is aware is already *it;* it is already perfect and cannot become anything other than its already perfect nature.

This is why many spiritual seekers get confused because they continue to seek enlightenment as if it were some mystical state. Enlightenment is not a special experience that one can achieve after a certain amount of spiritual work—whether in the form of mediation, prayer, or self-inquiry. It can be the hardest thing or the easiest thing depending on the perspective. If one is seeking it as an objective experience, then one will take a thousand lifetimes. But if you realize that the eternal is without objective quality and is only here and now—then it is instant.

There was a story where after a Zen master heard his student saying, "I'm meditating to become a Buddha," the master started to polish a rock. Upon seeing that, the student asked, "why are you polishing a rock?" The master answered: "I'm trying to make a mirror," the student followed, "how can you make a mirror by polishing a rock?" Then the master replied, "how can you become a Buddha by meditating?"

> "The paradox about waking up—I mean the ordinary kind of waking up that occurred to you and me this morning—is that you can't make it happen, yet it's inevitable. The same holds true spiritually. You can't wish, pray, beg, force, or meditate yourself awake."[1] (Deepak Chopra)

Many teachers have tried to teach spiritual practices like yoga in order to get the seeker to attain some kind of divine experience like kundalini—in which cosmic energy is awakened at the base of one's spine. All yogic practices—whether it's Bhakti, Jnana, Karma, or Kriya—are just a practice that can enhance your energies and your experience of life. However, a kundalini or a spiritual experience is not enlightenment. All experiences —no matter how mystical or how special—must still occur within consciousness for them to be knowable. Otherwise, they would have no existential value. So do not be fascinated by any particular experience. Instead, be fascinated by the knower of experience—the fact that experiencing is knowable is the greatest miracle.

Enlightenment cannot make you a perfect human being who will always do the right thing and is blissful in all circumstances. All of that is a change in the world of form; the formless is already here in the now; when spiritual seekers don't realize this, they will end up pursuing enlightenment for their entire life and ultimately get nowhere. You could become a Saint, a Monk, or a Pope—you could live your entire life doing only "good" deeds, but all you have done is adhered to a pattern. Enlightenment is your very self; you do not have to do something to become it. "Wherever you are is the entry point" (Kabir)

> "Truth is not a reward for good behaviour, nor a prize for passing some tests. It cannot be brought about. It is the primary, the unborn, the ancient source of all that is. You are eligible because you *are*. You need not merit truth."[2] (Nisargadatta Maharaj)

When the mind strongly seeks a particular experience—after having fantasized about it for a great deal—then sooner or later, it will manifest that experience from its own fantasies. If one thinks that enlightenment is like some kind of hysteria, a sense of oneness, or a meeting with God, then after enough spiritual practices—like chanting, meditation, or psychedelic drugs—you can get hysterical or hallucinate the God that you have imagined. However, all experiences are ephemeral—whatever that has a beginning will inevitably have an end—so you need to seek it over and over again. Enlightenment is the recognition of which has no beginning and ending; enlightenment is not an unending mystical experience.

If someone has a very dense pain-body and have been trapped in their convoluted thought structures for a long time, and then when they realize that they are not what they thought they were after all this time, a significant amount of tensions and repressed energies can suddenly get released from their body. The release may be accompanied by uncontrollable laughter or tears or a sense of union with the universe. Such an experience can become very memorable, and so people may think that the experience itself was enlightenment. This is a mistake. The experience was not enlightenment; all it was was just a pleasant experience. Many people will go back to their egoic selves and ignore their true nature after having it.

When someone has been caught in their thought loops for a long time, even an awakening experience can be quite rare; it sometimes happens when you have witnessed beauty in nature or something wonderful. And at that moment, thinking has suddenly stopped, and awareness has expanded; you were the thought, but now you are observing the thought. When you're out of your mind, you see that everything is as it should be, and an overwhelming joy can take over you.

That's why some people are fascinated with psychedelic drugs, because it can be an easy and powerful way to get snapped out of a thought loop that they have been caught in for a long time. Psychedelics are helpful in the beginning when you are completely stuck. However, if you are relying on it for a pleasurable experience again and again, then it just becomes another drug. Similarly, spiritual teachers and books are just signposts and tools in your journey—don't get stuck on them—otherwise, you will miss the road. And once you have arrived, you don't need the tools anymore. If you keep carrying them after realization, then they can become a hindrance. After you are out of a dark cave, you don't need to carry a torch around everywhere.

Typically, an awakening experience will not completely free the individual from their egoic patterns. There are times where a very powerful experience has completely liberated an individual, but such experiences are often rare. For most people, their old patterns will take over after some time. It usually takes a series of seeing into their true nature—along with maintaining a spiritual practice—will most of their egoic structures completely dissolve, and when that happens, their inner state becomes very pleasant. This is why many spiritual teachers do not aim for enlightenment because it's often too abstract. Instead, they aim for happiness. Gautama Buddha was able to gather a large following to his teachings because he was not aiming for God-realization or enlightenment. Instead, he was aiming for the end of suffering. Many people resonated with that because they understood suffering, but they did not understand enlightenment. "Enlightenment is the end of suffering." (The Buddha)

To explain enlightenment in more plain terms, it has more to do with how much you are abiding as awareness, and how much egoic structure has fallen away. And that can only take place in the now. You may have had an extraordinary experience 5 years ago, but today—as you are now—are you an ego or awareness? And that's the question. If you have doubts, then your seeing was not clear. The seeing into your true nature must clear away all doubts, because you cannot have a doubt about what you are; this is the most fundamental truth of existence.

Therefore, enlightenment is not a past accomplishment, so you shouldn't use your past enlightenment experience to escape your responsibilities for how you are now. If you are aware of your inner negativities, then you must face them. This does not mean that you need to judge yourself and try to be a better person, because that's just adhering to another mechanical pattern. You cannot be good by *trying* to be good, you can only discover *that* which is already good, and then you become fresh and spontaneous. "The greatest error of a man is to think that he is weak by nature, evil by nature. Every man is divine and strong in his real nature. What are weak and evil are his habits, his desires and thoughts, but not himself." (Ramana Maharshi)

Enlightened masters may describe their experience as having a more silent mind or being more loving, joyous, or non-reactive. Those descriptions are only meant to give you some pointers as to what enlightenment looks like, so if you absolutely need something to measure your progress, you can use it. However, such qualities are really the product of enlightenment, so do not mistake the consequences of the understanding with the understanding itself. You do not reach enlightenment by trying to quiet your mind or being more happy. Instead, you can only be what you are, so it's more of a negation of existing effort rather than an accumulation of new efforts. "Enlightenment is total emptiness of mind. There is nothing you can do to get it. Any effort you make can only be an obstruction to it." (Ramesh Balsekar)

Because the absolute truth cannot be told, the closest that the teachers could communicate about it is to say what it is not. That's why the spiritual teachings are called "non-duality," as in "not two." They cannot say that there is one, because one is still fundamentally a concept, and reality is beyond all concepts. There was a Zen story where a boy was imitating a Zen master's teaching by raising a single finger in front of people, and then one day, when the master cut off that finger, the boy

YANHAO HUANG

became enlightened.

PARADOXES OF ENLIGHTENMENT

The conundrum that the spiritual teachers face is that, on the one hand, they are trying to teach you to find happiness and end your divisiveness, while on the other, they are trying to teach you to abide as what you already are. Those two notions appear to be in contradiction. Because if I'm miserable, how can I be happy by continuing to remain as I am—which is miserable? And this is why there's so much confusion in spiritual teachings. So some teachers only focus on one side of the teaching; they will teach you as if you are in control of your life, so you need to deal with your thoughts and emotions until your energy is harmonious. While other teachers will focus on the other side and will teach you that there is nothing you can really do, because whatever you think you are doing comes from the ego—which is the problem. If I feel proud because of how egoless I am, or much longer I can mediate compared to others, then I am not ending my antagonism. Instead, I am only strengthening my ego. That is why even amongst enlightened masters, you will see contradictory statements.

A simple explanation for the seemingly paradoxical advice is that while the idea is to go from suffering to happiness, but the way to get there is not by *trying* to get there. When we are in ego-consciousness, we are always trying to be something better, and it is this conflict and striving that is the problem. We are not miserable because we are okay with being miserable. We are actually miserable because we are trying to be something else; if we can fully accept our misery, then our misery will go. To paraphrase Eckhart Tolle: to be aware of our own insanity is the arising sanity, and the beginning of transcendence.

When we are conscious of our essence as consciousness itself, we don't need a technique anymore. We cannot actually be what we are not, so we are always aware regardless of what we do. But before our recognition, we need some technique to get to the technique-less state, which is another paradoxical situation that the teachers face. While the truth is that you cannot really be anything other than consciousness, and that the dream character is not really in control, so misery is equally valid in existence as happiness. However, in the realm of the relative, it is better to have a more pleasant dream, and so you should move towards that while you still feel like you are in control. That's why here in the dream world, the techniques and teachings are valuable, and people venerate the wise and the knowledgeable.

The techniques toward enlightenment include meditation, and conducting yourself consciously —as in not losing yourself as awareness while going through your day. Some techniques suggest that you practice concentrating on a particular object or thought, so that your mind can be more disciplined and less erratic. While other techniques suggest that you cease concentration, and instead just allow whatever that comes into your consciousness to be there—that way, your mind will settle down and be attentive on its own. "When meditation is mastered, the mind is unwavering like the flame of a lamp in a windless place."[3] (*Bhagavad Gita*)

You can experiment with the different techniques and see what works for you. There are times where you may find it helpful to drop all activities and meditate for 12+ hours a day, while other times you may want to just forget all practice and see what happens. Learning is a moment-to-moment process. You don't need to be locked into any particular method. What is true for one person in a particular situation is not true for another person in a different situation.

On the flip side—in the realm of the absolute— there's really no teaching nor learning, because teachers can only teach you knowledge, but they cannot teach you what you are. You are already-

that, and you just need to recognize it. Even the recognition is not really up to you as the dream character. Ironically, once you sincerely know that you cannot make it happen, and have absolutely let go of all control, then you will see that the universal Consciousness is really orchestrating everything from the start. It is not the dream character that wakes up. It is the dreamer—consciousness—that awakens to its own nature. The only difference—if you want to call it a difference—is you have the understanding that you are in a dream —similar to lucid dreaming—so you don't need to take everything so seriously. But this does not necessarily mean that your dream will drastically change, because you will still experience the dream the same way you have always experienced it.

The enlightened state is simply, and always, the Now—it is just whatever you are experiencing at this very moment. Only thoughts can seem to cloud it if you give them too much importance— like doubting your own nature or expecting a special experience—but even so, they still only take place in Consciousness, in the Now. This is why some called it the gateless gate, because there is no actual barrier to insight. As Rumi said, "I have lived on the lip of insanity, wanting to know reasons, knocking on a door. It opens. I've been knocking from the inside." And to paraphrase St. Francis of Assisi: what we are looking for is where we are looking from. God is the only one who is aware. Enlightenment is realizing that you are God itself. Do not get a sense of superiority over this, because that comes from the ego. True recognition of God is recognizing that all else is God also.

Do not be fooled when some spiritual teachers say that you need to reach some kind of super-consciousness state. They may say that to concep-tualize certain things, but ultimately there are no different levels of consciousness. As long as a state is knowable, it can only appear in the same con-sciousness that had always been there—which is always here and now.

> "This moment is not life waiting to happen, goals waiting to be achieved, words waiting to be spoken, connections waiting to be made, re-grets waiting to evaporate, aliveness waiting to be felt, enlightenment waiting to be gained. No. Nothing is waiting. This is it. This moment is life."[4] (Jeff Foster)

For the purposes of teaching spirituality, we need to distinguish those that are enlightened from those that are not so that we can give a defin-ition of enlightenment. However, once enlighten-ment has happened, such a distinction will fall away. You cannot separate yourself from those "unenlightened" people as that will contradict your understanding. "What is the Ultimate Under-standing? That there is no one to understand anything" (Ramesh Balsekar). That's why the enlightened masters will not refer to themselves as enlightened. Enlightenment is often a label given to the master by other people, not the master themself. So don't get caught up with the labels, and instead, focus on the journey. Once your energy has transformed to a certain degree, people may take notice, and it's okay when somebody else says that you are enlightened. However, it's foolish to undergo a spiritual journey just so that you can declare yourself to be enlightened.

Although you are the timeless and the infinite, whether you know it or not, knowing it will bring about a new mind. If you were sitting on a billion dollars, would you say that you are rich if you don't know it? If you realize that everything in existence is fundamentally you, then you will not need to be taught to be kind to others, to care for the environment, to end violence, and so on. You will do them effortlessly because it's in your nature to do so.

We cannot deny the value of ignorance also because the forgetting of our true nature is intentionally done by God to make our dreams more exciting. But eventually, God will return back to her own self. We can see the oscillations of inward and outward movement in all of life—from breathing to mating to the span of a sentient being. When a being comes into existence, there's the outward movement of consciousness in which it becomes fascinated with form—as it acquires and achieves more in the worldly dimension—but toward the end of one's life, consciousness starts its inward movement—as the body deteriorates and returns back to its source.

On a macro level, the world as a whole is becoming more conscious. We can see that consciousness is expanding its range of expression through the increasing complexity of forms. If we are attuned to the spiritual dimension of life, we can see that more and more people are interested in living consciously, and spiritual awakening is becoming a more common phenomenon. Many spiritual teachings that used to be obscure are now more popular, and spiritual teachers like Eckhart Tolle and Sadhguru are recognized across the globe. Ultimately, the universe is conspiring with itself to move every form towards enlightenment because all is one.

POST-ENLIGHTENMENT

After a powerful awakening experience, you may notice that you no longer feel the need to repress all your emotions. So when your resistances drop—all your latent pains and other unconscious material can start to surface themselves rapidly. Many people can get so overwhelmed that they end up re-identifying with their mind again so they can avoid the darker aspects of themselves. Some people will try to rush into a relationship or a job to keep themselves occupied. And some minds can latch onto the self-image of being "enlightened," which can give rise to another ego and subsequently block one's spiritual progress.

However, when awareness rises to a certain degree within you, you will find it much more painful not to act according to the truth. Because you can see through your own biases—you know that there's nothing which makes your dream character more right than anyone else—as all perspectives are equally valid. Thus, you can no longer hold any belief to be the absolute truth. Before awakening, it's easy to turn a blind eye to your own issues and put the blame on others, but now you are compelled to look at the fallacies of your own logic.

When you start to distance yourself from your ego, you get to see how silly you are. And this can be a very disconcerting experience for many—as you can no longer believe in the things you say— it's almost like you are inhabiting a foreign body. All the motivations you used to have are now gone; what used to make you happy can no longer make you happy. Your ego desires—like money and achievements—now hold no meaning. Your plan in life is completely falling apart. You don't know what you want to do nor what you want to be; you are completely lost. You see that everyone else has a plan and is working towards it—as they are climbing the corporate ladder and getting married —but you find yourself completely losing interest in all of it.

You may even try to go back to your old ways, like starting a new relationship or business—but no matter what you do—they just don't provide the same thrill. The drive and conviction that you used to have are simply gone. Once you have peaked at the truth, you can never fully turn away; it's like trying to get back into the Matrix after being un-plugged—you can no longer fool yourself with the same illusions again. You find yourself in a free fall, unable to grasp at anything—you can't be the ego, but you are also not awareness. And when awareness has not fully flowered within you, your inner state is not naturally happy, but you are also no longer able to enjoy what used to make you happy. Eventually, you will find life to be utterly meaningless, and you may sink into a deep depression as a result. Some describe this phase as the dark night of the soul, and it can last anywhere between an hour to several years.

During this phase, you may find that you can no longer hold onto certain relationships because your consciousness has outgrown them by too much. When two people's state of consciousness is too far apart, they will separate like "oil and water"—as analogized by Eckhart Tolle. When a relationship needs to end, then let it end. Do not cling to it; you need to let whatever that has to end to end—and those things can also include your job, identity, belief, and religion.

Consciousness will rearrange your external circumstances to reflect your inner state. You have to die to the old to invite the new. If you can choose transformation, then choose it. However, for some, it will be chosen for them—they are forced to evolve. Like the metamorphosis of a caterpillar—the caterpillar does not want to become the butterfly, it wants to stay intact, but nevertheless, a butterfly will happen when it needs to happen.

Your first priority in the dark phase of the spiritual

journey is to not escape yourself—do not try to distract yourself by filling up your schedule with activities. Instead, be willing to face all aspects of yourself—your biases, your wrongs, your guilts, your embarrassments, and your inadequacies—no matter how uncomfortable they may be.

Your focus should be on managing your thoughts and emotions. Because they are the closest things to you—relatively speaking—that you can control while you still feel like having some sense of control. Thus, take as much responsibility as you can in your life and don't put the blame on anybody. If someone insults you, instead of building up hate for them, you look at yourself and see why they did that to you. If you conclude that it was not your problem—then look at your thoughts and emotions—see if there is hate, anger, and antagonism. If there is, you need to deal with it; what others do is their business. You do as much as you can to nurture your consciousness, and leave whatever that is outside of your control. Why worry about what you can't control anyway? "Save all your energies and time for breaking the wall your mind has built around you."[5] (Nisargadatta Maharaj)

Yes, this book has previously said that the dream character is not really in control. Still, you don't have to try to feel like that in your day-to-day moments—that won't work if you try to force it—it has to come about naturally. More realistically speaking, you can simply look at your dream character as having limited control and approach life that way. Sometimes the simplest understanding is the most effective; you have some influence over how your life will turn out, but there's also a large portion of it beyond your control—like your genetics, early life circumstances, and so on. So just put all your energy into your efforts, and forget all else. Otherwise, the anxiety that you develop by trying to control what you can't control can really stifle your efforts. However, you must also be careful not to avoid responsibility in what you should take responsibility for. Many people try to use the absolute view to escape their responsibilities; they believe that their unfortunate circumstances can justify their mediocre efforts—this is not the right approach. You can always do your best, even in the direst circumstances. "You have power over your mind - not outside events. Realize this, and you will find strength." (Marcus Aurelius)

Physical suffering is inevitable in life, but psychological suffering is mostly self-inflicted. If you cease your resistance to life, then you can handle anything that life throws at you. You could even be tortured, but if you cooperate with the situation instead of feeling "this should not happen to me," then there would be no suffering—and some may even find pleasure in it. This is why there are people like Ascetics and Masochists who willingly inflict pain and suffering onto themselves. In Victor Frankl's *Man's Search for Meaning*, he was able to endure the suffering of the concentration camps because he found meaning within himself.

In earlier spiritual traditions, it typically takes a seeker about 10+ years of practice under a guru to reach full liberation, so that one can be carefully guided through the turmoils of the journey. But in modern times, such methods are not practical. Most people will not have the means to study under a guru for that long, so the teachings must be delivered in a much more accessible and direct manner. Most of the work now falls on the individual—you are solely responsible for your spiritual progression. However, you don't really need a guru because Consciousness is already within you; you can learn to trust in life, and it will always guide you to the truth. "Everything in the world was my Guru." (Ramana Maharshi)

> "Life will give you whatever experience is most helpful for the evolution of your consciousness. How do you know this is the experience you need? Because this is the experience you are having at the moment."[6] (Eckhart Tolle)

Therefore, work with each moment as if you had created it because, in a way, you have—just like your dreams—the dream is you. The limited mind will never grasp how the macro universe works—but each moment is carefully being orchestrated by Consciousness to put on this grand show. "Life can only be understood backwards, but it must be lived forwards" (Søren Kierkegaard)

If you absolutely have to know how much you have progressed spiritually, you can see how you conduct yourself in actual challenging situations —like when something tragic is happening to you —see if you get flustered by such events. Your reaction shows whether your understanding is merely intellectual or if it has truly taken root. If knowing your true nature to be God is just a belief, then you will constantly be disturbed. However, if your egoic energies have been completely dissolved, then you cannot be swayed by any circumstance.

Toward the end of the dark night of the soul, you may find yourself flipping back and forth between ego and awareness—sometimes very rapidly—you find yourself absolutely ecstatic at times, but you also find yourself acting out old patterns. Eventually, you won't even care about all the flipping back and forth—you start to relinquish control to that as well; you remain as awareness, as a nothing, and let the phenomenal world do as it may —you let existence take care of the rest of it. "Whoever brought me here will have to take me home." (Rumi)

During this period, a more abiding enlightenment experience may happen—where all doubts can be shattered. For some, the experience can be quite mystical. There was a fictional story written by

Hermann Hesse, where two lifelong friends—Siddhartha and Govinda—has been seeking liberation for their entire life. They've then gone their separate ways, and Siddhartha eventually found realization, but Govinda has not. When Govinda reunited with Siddhartha toward their twilight years, Govinda suddenly saw the oneness of all life:

> "He [Govinda] no longer saw the face of his friend Siddhartha, instead he saw other faces, many, a long sequence, a flowing river of faces, of hundreds, of thousands, which all came and disappeared, and yet all seemed to be there simultaneously, which all constantly changed and renewed themselves ... [H]e saw the face of a new-born child, red and full of wrinkles, distorted from crying—he saw the face of a murderer, he saw him plunging a knife into the body of another person—he saw, in the same second, this criminal in bondage, kneeling and his head being chopped off by the executioner with one blow of his sword—he saw the bodies of men and women, naked in positions and cramps of frenzied love—he saw corpses stretched out, motionless, cold, void—he saw the heads of animals, of boars, of crocodiles, of elephants, of bulls, of birds—he saw gods, saw Krishna, saw Agni—he saw all of these figures and faces in a thousand relationships with one another, each one helping the other, loving it, hating it, destroying it, giving re-birth

to it, each one was a will to die, a passionately painful confession of transitoriness, and yet none of them died, each one only transformed, was always re-born, received evermore a new face... they were all constantly covered by something thin, without individuality of its own, but yet existing, like a ... mask of water, and this mask was smiling, ... this smile of oneness above the flowing forms ..."[7] (*Siddhartha*)

Once you see the nature of yourself, you will see that everything is made out of you, but when you have even let go of the concept of you, then you will simply see everything as they are.

"Before one studies Zen, mountains are mountains and waters are waters; after a first glimpse into the truth of Zen, mountains are no longer mountains and waters are no longer waters; after enlightenment, mountains are once again mountains and waters once again waters." (Dōgen)

Do not abandon your spiritual journey after enlightenment, because the mind and worldly desires will always be enticing, so stay vigilant and always be true to yourself. "Before enlightenment, chop wood, carry water. After enlightenment, chop wood, carry water." (Zen Master)

As you develop spiritually, you may find yourself needing less and less sleep because your mind no longer consumes so much energy during the day. You may also find drastic changes in your habits, like the people you associate with, the foods you consume, and the activities you partake in—no need to be alarmed by all this. As long as they happen on their own and not forced, then it is all part of the transformation process.

For certain individuals, they may find themself in possession of certain—perhaps even supernatural —abilities. They may have visions of how the future will turn out or have healing powers—where others get their emotional distress or physical illnesses dissolved from being in their presence. They may not even be aware of such abilities until they've witnessed a certain number of coincidences.

In the yogic tradition, the spiritual powers or miracles are called siddhis. The masters are known to perform supernatural feats like teleportation, invisibility, levitation, astral travel, and so on. The siddhi powers may sometimes happen to individuals, or they may not. However, if you do find yourself with such abilities, the important thing is to not take pride in it—many can find themselves developing a God complex over it, as they think that the powers can somehow prove that they are spiritually superior to others. That's why you don't see the masters demonstrate their power, and so the siddhis are hardly mainstream as a result. Another reason is obviously that many of them turn out to be just myths.

There's no denying that the spiritual powers are nice to have—they show the power of consciousness and prove the interconnectedness of all things. But in the modern world, they are more like a magic trick, because what would be the point of levitating or walking on water—when we can just use airplanes and boats?

What is more important in life is how you handle yourself. If you can go through the traumas of life unscathed and have brought kindness to the world, that is a much greater accomplishment than levitating. Do you want to be Gandhi or David Blaine? If you start performing siddhis, then all you will get is to have people interested in spiritual powers rather than the truth of existence; people will try to do magic tricks rather than ending their own divisiveness. So focus on your true nature and forget all else. "Your own Self-Realization is the greatest service you can render the world." (Ramana Maharshi)

PARADOXES OF THE GAME OF LIFE

After you have abided as the timeless awareness for some time, you may start to gain insights into life. You will see how the real workings of the universe are paradoxical to the conventional mind.

You see that when you have fully let go of control, then you really have it, because when you are no longer in conflict with everything, then everything obeys you. Life is at its best when you go about it effortlessly; the more effort you use, the more you are swimming against the stream because you only perpetuate what you resist.

Freedom is not about having more choices. Freedom is free from choice. When you want more choices, you are actually inviting more conflict—like energy being pulled toward multiple directions. When there's a clear choice, then paradoxically, there would be no choice. When the right things happen on their own—that's true freedom.

You may think freedom means to be rich and so free from having to work and being able to do what you want and date who you want—this is freedom in a conceptual sense but not in an existential sense. At this very moment—in your particular circumstance—are those options possible? If not, then the imagined scenarios are conflicting with what you can do right now. You don't reach financial freedom by dreaming about it and demeaning your current circumstance because you don't have it. You reach your destiny by aligning yourself with the present moment in every step of the journey. So seek to cooperate with the universe instead of fighting against it.

When you cooperate with the universe, you will not feel bitter towards rejection because that's a decision the universe has made. However, when you get multiple offers, then you have to make the decision. And who has more intelligence? You or the universe? Our mind will always be limited, and the universe is always infinite, so trust in the universe, and do not be afraid when the doors close on you—you are always on the right path.

When you trust in life, then life starts to become extremely simple—you were trying to go through life as if it were a video game, but really it's just a movie. You don't need to follow an elaborate plan to aim for a certain outcome. Instead, you can just deal with the present moment—and that's enough. You can never be stuck in the present—you may be stuck in a projected scenario, but the present will always flow. Even if you have no idea what to do, the present will still work itself out. When you live this way, you will feel like driving without one foot on the brake; you are free from carrying around a 500-pound weight—that is, the ego—everywhere you go.

"Paradox as it may seem, we likewise find life meaningful only when we have seen that it is without purpose, and know the 'mystery of the universe' only when we are convinced that we know nothing about it at all."[8] (Alan Watts)

When you are free from your mind, you will not need any authority or advice to go about your life. You discover that your default state will always yield the best result. There's nothing you can do to be natural—any effort you make only makes you more mechanical.

People who live with death are the most alive—when you die every moment to all your past beliefs and identities, you become fresh and spontaneous. When you have no need for security, then you have true security. When you have no fear of doing the wrong thing, then that energy itself is transformative and ecstatic.

Most people are in the pursuit of happiness, as they are trying to fulfill certain conditions in order to reach it. This is backward; it is only when you are happy, then the desired conditions will follow. If we can be joyful in any circumstance, we can do things out of joy instead of fear, and we will be much more productive as a result.

"In order to fulfil the desire for happiness, most people engage in a relentless search in the realm of objects, substances, activities, states of mind and relationships. This search also takes the form of resistance to whomever or whatever is perceived to jeopardize our happiness. ...

The activities of seeking and resisting are an inevitable expression of the sense of lack or suffering that underlies them. However, most of us never question the origin of our suffering, so busy are we escaping the discomfort of it through the acquisition of objects... If we do question it, we usually attribute it to the absence of the object or experience that we seek or the presence of the situation we are attempting to avoid and, as a result, never fully trace it back to its original cause.

Our belief that happiness is dependent on objective experience is not altogether without foundation, and hence its almost universal allure, for every time a desired object is acquired or an unpleasant situation successfully avoided, happiness is indeed briefly experienced.

However, although the acquisition or avoidance of the object or situation puts a temporary end to the suffering that underlies it and, as a result, brings about a brief moment of happiness, it does not uproot it or bring it to a permanent end. It simply masks it.

... As a result, most people set out again in pursuit or rejection of some form of objective experience in the hopes of repeating the experience of happiness. In this way we become addicted to the endless cycle of lack, seeking and temporary fulfilment that characterises most people's lives, and to which Henry David Thoreau referred when he said that most people 'lead lives of quiet desperation'."[9] (Rupert Spira, *Being Aware of Being Aware*)

You can never find happiness in another. You can only find it within yourself. When someone makes you happy, the happiness is not coming from them; it is coming from you. Paraphrasing Sadhguru: you have merely used them as a key to unlock something that was already within you. But such a key is unnecessary because you have made up the lock; abandon the lock, and the key is no longer needed. When you are not naturally happy yourself—nobody can make you happy. They may temporarily cover up your lack, but sooner or later, problems will start. Two halves can never make a whole; a half will always be a half, only a whole can remain a whole. Only when you can be happy alone, then can you be happy with another.

> "The capacity to be alone is the capacity to love. It may look paradoxical to you, but it's not. It is an existential truth: only those people who are capable of being alone are capable of love, of sharing, of going into the deepest core of another person--without possessing the other, without becoming dependent on the other, without reducing the other to a thing, and without becoming addicted to the other. They allow the other absolute freedom, because they know that if the other leaves, they will be as happy as they are now. Their happiness cannot be taken by the other, because it is not given by the other." (Osho)

When you have a desire, you become a slave to it. Your life and happiness revolve around attaining it. The object of desire never contains any happiness; it's just an object. When you attain it, the object of desire will change because your desire will latch onto another. The desire is the problem —not the object. How can something external be responsible for something that is inherently internal? Whether you are miserable from not satisfying your desires or happy from fulfilling them— regardless, it's happening within you. So we must recognize the source of happiness—the emotions are coming from us; if we are not happy, then we are the problem—not outside events. And the happiness that we experience from getting the desired object is actually caused by the cessation of our desire. But, we falsely attribute it to an object —that's why our happiness is short-lived because our desires will start up again. As long as there's desire, we will be trapped in the world of form and thus subject to the laws of duality—gains and loss, highs and lows.

> "So long as the soul of man is encased in one, two, or three body-containers, sealed tightly with the corks of ignorance and desires, he cannot merge with the sea of Spirit. When the gross physical receptacle is destroyed by the hammer of death, the other two coverings-astral and causal-still remain to prevent the soul from consciously joining the Omnipresent Life. When desirelessness is attained through wisdom, its power disintegrates the two remaining vessels. The tiny human soul emerges, free at last; it is one with the Measureless Amplitude."[10] (Paramhansa Yogananda, *Autobiography of a Yogi*)

In some sense, the world is a game in which consciousness is trapped in various dimensions of form. It is working through its desires or its blocked energies, in other words, to return back to its original self. Pieces of consciousness are reincarnating into different forms in different lives to experience different dreams—until all of its desires are fulfilled or evaporated. And when that happens, it returns back to its original state—the formless—like your existence in deep sleep. From this perspective, no one can truly be enlightened because the evidence is that they are in a body. And as long as there's a body, there will inevitably be desire—the desire for food, for shelter, for sex, and so on. True enlightenment is when all desires have perished, and there's only the formless left.

But don't try to stop your desires because that's impossible—all you will do is desire to not to desire—which is still a desire nevertheless—and you cannot get out of this predicament. For now, when you are in a form—you are here to enjoy the dream, so just enjoy it. And when you reincarnate into another form or realm, you can enjoy those also. Each individual evolves at their own pace. Remember, your essence is not reincarnating. It is the dream character that is reincarnating—essentially mind-stuff.

To provide a metaphor often used by Rupert Spira —each mind is like a whirlpool in the river of consciousness—or a localization of consciousness in other words. When the body comes to an end, the mind's residual energy disperses and can entangle with other energy ripples to form a new whirlpool —which is a new mind. Although the new mind is a completely different person, just like the person you dream up in your sleep is completely different. Nevertheless, don't think that your spiritual work is all for nothing because your energy does carry forward and can affect subsequent whirlpools formed in consciousness. A loving mind will resonate with other loving minds to form a more spiritually evolved being the next time around. Every action has a ripple effect toward the entirety of consciousness. The observation that there is a linkage between lives is what gave rise to the concept of reincarnation and karma in various religious and spiritual traditions.

At the end of the day, it doesn't really matter how reality is—there may be multiverses, astral realms, simulations, or whatever else of existence there is. You only need to recognize the dimension within you that is already desire-less, and rest as that. Your deep tendencies, or Vāsanās in yogic terms, will dissolve on their own. When your consciousness has expanded to a certain degree, you will have a conscious choice of when and how to leave the body. When the time comes, if you go into the void consciously, you won't be reincarnated back to the world of form and subject to further suffering—you will be merged completely with God. And that's the ultimate ecstasy, the ultimate purpose of existence in some sense. You don't need to fear and resist death—when it comes, you can fully let go and go gentle into that good night.

However, don't think that death will get you to God—death only ends the body—if the mind is not ready, then your unconscious material will bring you back to Saṃsāra again and again until all of your issues are resolved. You cannot escape yourself through death. You must find liberation in life —you can only reach nirvana through Saṃsāra. The First Law of Thermodynamics states that energy cannot be created nor destroyed—it can only be transformed. Therefore, either you transform into the divine, or you will transform into another form.

It is only when you realize that there's nothing outside of you that can make you happy, you can discover your inner Being that is inherently happy. And that Being is the void itself, you can never fill the emptiness within—the emptiness is you; "nothing can make you happy until Nothing can make you happy." (Jeff Foster)

"Happiness is your nature. It is not wrong to desire it. What is wrong is seeking it outside when it is inside" (Ramana Maharshi). To be happy is how the Law of Attraction really works. When your true nature as happiness takes over, then synchronicities happen, then things happen your way. When you no longer need anything, then everything will be given. When you are so abundant with love and joy, then you will not be concerned about receiving them. And instead, you will give all that you are, and the universe will respond accordingly. "The home is the abiding place; in the home is reality; the home helps to attain Him Who is real. So stay where you are, and all things shall come to you in time." (Kabir)

Attention is your true nature, so always take the watchful position when approaching life; it is not a passive position—there is tremendous power in that neutrality. "Anything in this existence will yield to you only if you pay substantial attention to it" (Sadhguru). You may have noticed this yourself, when you have paid attention to a problem that you were facing—even if you don't think you will ever solve it—but as long as you kept on paying attention to it, the solution usually turns up. The paradox is that the more conscious you become, the more things become automatic—not automatic in the sense of unconscious autopilot, but automatic in the sense of things happening spontaneously. The more you trust in life, the less you need to exert your control over things, because they will simply unfold in your favour.

> "Even though you try to put people under control, it is impossible. You cannot do it. The best way to control people is to encourage them to be mischievous. Then they will be in control in a wider sense. ... To ignore them is not good. That is the worst policy. The second worst is trying to control them. The best one is to watch them, just to watch them, without trying to control them."[11] (Shunryu Suzuki)

So face the world of form but remain as the formless. "Know the male, yet keep to the female: receive the world in your arms"[12] (Lao Tzu). When you have lost your essence, then everything needs to be enforced. But when you abide as awareness, then all the right things will come about naturally.

> "When the great Tao is forgotten, goodness and piety appear.
> When the body's intelligence declines, cleverness and knowledge step forth.
> When there is no peace in the family, filial piety begins.
> When the country falls into chaos, patriotism is born.
>
> Throw away holiness and wisdom, and people will be a hundred times happier.
> Throw away morality and justice, and people will do the right thing.
> Throw away industry and profit, and there won't be any thieves.
> If these three aren't enough, just stay at the center of the circle and let all things take their course."[13]
> (Lao Tzu, *Tao Te Ching*)

TO THE BEYOND

Two of the greatest literary works were the book *The Heart of Darkness*, written by Joseph Conrad, and the movie *Apocalypse Now*, directed by Francis Ford Coppola. The screenplay of *Apocalypse Now* was made based on Conrad's book. In the story, the protagonist must travel up a river to reach the objective of his quest—Kurtz. The river is a metaphorical journey from civilization to barbarism. It can also symbolize the psychological transformation that the characters go through as they get closer to the heart of darkness—as embodied by Kurtz.

If one can fully face the savagery of the human psyche without losing one's sanity, then one can overcome the heart of darkness. The people who cannot face it will descend into madness like the natives and soldiers up the river. As for the so-called civilized people back home in America, civilization has merely obscured their savagery. Nevertheless, their savagery is still there, so it is expressed in another form—like being caught up in comparisons and antagonizing one another for their differences. Such inhumanity is no different than the inhumanity embodied by the savages up the river.

We have a similar journey as well. Although we may not travel up a real river, our hidden psychological traumas are what we must face to reach our own heart of darkness. We must fully acknowledge our hatred, jealousy, fears, and hollowness before we can overcome them. We must go through the mind rabbit hole to find ourselves beyond our conceptual prison. When we expose the darkness and distortions of our own psyche to the light of awareness, then we will bring it to an end. However, if we do not face ourselves and continue to run away from ourselves, then we will be lost in the Wonderland of our minds. We will remain as an ego and perpetuate our divisiveness and negativity as a result.

> "There is no coming to consciousness without pain. People will do anything, no matter how absurd, in order to avoid facing their own soul. One does not become enlightened by imagining figures of light, but by making the darkness conscious." (Carl Jung)

Apotheosis is defined as the divination of a human being to a God. This does not mean that the human being has elevated themself to some kind of a super being that possesses special powers—that's a misconception of apotheosis. Divination is not an additive process. It is the elimination of all that is not original to you until only the divine is left. As Ramana Maharshi said: "Realisation is not acquisition of anything new nor is it a new faculty. It is only removal of all camouflage."

When your consciousness is no longer divided into you and others, good and bad, higher and lower self, then there's no more division and so no more friction. You have become *that* which has no opposite; you are neither everything nor nothing, but also is simultaneously everything and nothing; you are *beyond* what concepts can capture. As you continue to abide as your true nature, you will transform unconsciousness into consciousness— transmute iron into gold, ego into God—and that is true apotheosis.

If you enjoyed this book, please consider leaving a short review on Amazon. Thank you!

ENDNOTES

Chapter One

1. Maltz, Maxwell. *Psycho-Cybernetics: A New Way to Get More Living out of Life*. Reprint ed. (New York: Pocket Books, 1969), preface.

2. Pirsig, Robert. *Zen and the Art of Motorcycle Maintenance: An Inquiry Into Values*. Reprint ed. (HarperCollins e-books, 2009), ch. 7.

3. Suzuki, Shunryu. *Zen Mind, Beginner's Mind: 50th Anniversary Edition* (Shambhala, 2020), pt. 2 Communication.

4. Byrne, Rhonda. *The Secret*. 1st ed. (Atria Books/Beyond Words, 2007), ch. The Secret Revealed.

5. Byrne, Rhonda. *The Secret*. 1st ed. (Atria Books/Beyond Words, 2007), ch. How to Use The Secret.

6. Watts, Alan. *Out of Your Mind: Tricksters, Interdependence, and the Cosmic Game of Hide and Seek*. (Sounds True, 2017), ch. 2.

7. Watts, Alan. *The Way of Zen* (Vintage, 2011), pt. 2 ch. 1.

Chapter Two

1. Suzuki, Shunryu. *Zen Mind, Beginner's Mind: 50th Anniversary Edition* (Shambhala, 2020), pt. 2 Constancy.
2. Sadhguru. *Inner Engineering: A Yogi's Guide to Joy.* 1st ed. (Harmony, 2016), pt. 2 Mind.
3. Watts, Alan, and Chopra Deepak Md. *The Wisdom of Insecurity: A Message for an Age of Anxiety* (Vintage, 2011), ch. 3.
4. Watts, Alan. *Out of Your Mind: Tricksters, Interdependence, and the Cosmic Game of Hide and Seek.* (Sounds True, 2017), ch. 11.
5. Tolle, Eckhart. *A New Earth: Awakening to Your Life's Purpose.* Reprint ed. (Penguin, 2006), ch. 2.
6. Watts, Alan, and Chopra Deepak Md. *The Wisdom of Insecurity: A Message for an Age of Anxiety* (Vintage, 2011), Introduction.
7. Tolle, Eckhart. *The Power of Now: A Guide to Spiritual Enlightenment* (New World Library, 2010), ch. 7.
8. Friedman, Milton. *Capitalism and Freedom.* 1st ed. (Chicago: University of Chicago Press, 2003), ch. 8.
9. Tolle, Eckhart. *A New Earth: Awakening to Your Life's Purpose.* Reprint ed. (Penguin, 2006), ch. 2.
10. Tzu, Lao, and Stephen Mitchell. *Tao Te Ching: A New English Version.* Reprint ed.

(Harper Perennial, 2009), ch. 1.

11. Watts, Alan. *The Way of Zen* (Vintage, 2011), pt. 1 ch. 1.

Chapter Three

1. Watts, Alan. "We as Organism," https://alanwatts.org/1-4-5-we-as-organism/.

2. Mooji. *Vaster Than Sky, Greater Than Space: What You Are Before You Became* (Boulder: Sounds True, 2016), ch. 1.

3. Suzuki, Shunryu. *Zen Mind, Beginner's Mind: 50th Anniversary Edition* (Shambhala, 2020), Prologue.

4. Sadhguru. *Inner Engineering: A Yogi's Guide to Joy*. 1st ed. (Harmony, 2016), pt. 2 Mind.

5. Dispenza, Joe. *Becoming Supernatural: How Common People Are Doing the Uncommon*. (Carlsbad: Hay House Inc., 2017), ch. 3.

6. Krishnamurti, Jiddu, and Aldous Huxley. *The First and Last Freedom* (HarperCollins e-books, 2010), ch. 4.

7. Watts, Alan, and Chopra Deepak Md. *The Wisdom of Insecurity: A Message for an Age of Anxiety* (Vintage, 2011), ch. 5.

8. Maharaj, Nisargadatta, and Maurice Frydman. *I Am That*. 2nd American ed. (Durham: The Acorn Press, 2012), ch. 98.

9. Krishnamurti, Jiddu, and Aldous Huxley. *The First and Last Freedom* (HarperCollins e-books, 2010), Forward by Aldous Hux-

ley.

10. Pirsig, Robert. *Zen and the Art of Motorcycle Maintenance: An Inquiry Into Values*. Reprint ed. (HarperCollins e-books, 2009), ch. 13.

11. Ruiz, Don Miguel. *The Four Agreements: A Practical Guide to Personal Freedom* (Amber-Allen Publishing, 2018), ch. 1.

12. Krishnamurti, Jiddu, and Mary Lutyens. *Freedom from the Known* (San Francisco: HarperSanFrancisco, 2009), ch. 1.

13. Marx, Karl, and Friedrich Engels. *The Communist Manifesto*. (International Publishers Co, 2014), ch. I.

Chapter Four

1. Tzu, Lao, and Stephen Mitchell. *Tao Te Ching: A New English Version*. Reprint ed. (Harper Perennial, 2009), ch. 68.

2. Yogananda, Paramhansa. *Autobiography of a Yogi: The Original 1946 Edition*. 2nd ed. (Commerce: Crystal Clarity Publishers, 2005), ch. 12.

3. Tzu, Lao, and Stephen Mitchell. *Tao Te Ching: A New English Version*. Reprint ed. (Harper Perennial, 2009), ch. 69, 76.

4. Singer, Michael. *The Untethered Soul: The Journey Beyond Yourself*. 1st ed. (New Harbinger Publications, 2007), ch. 11.

5. Tolle, Eckhart. *The Power of Now: A Guide*

to Spiritual Enlightenment (Novato: New World Library, 2010), ch. 2.

6. Matthew 7:1 (New International Version)
7. Matthew 7:3 (New International Version)
8. Lama, Dalai. *The Art of Happiness: A Handbook for Living.* (Riverhead Books, 2009), ch. 2.
9. Krishnamurti, Jiddu, and Aldous Huxley. *The First and Last Freedom* (HarperCollins e-books, 2010), ch. 4.

Chapter Five

1. Krishnamurti, Jiddu, and Mary Lutyens. *Freedom from the Known* (San Francisco: HarperSanFrancisco, 2009), ch. 1.
2. Krishnamurti, Jiddu, and Mary Lutyens. *Freedom from the Known* (San Francisco: HarperSanFrancisco, 2009), ch. 2.
3. Holiday, Ryan. *Ego Is the Enemy.* (Portfolio, 2016), Introduction.
4. Jackson, Phil, and Hugh Delehanty. *Eleven Rings: The Soul of Success.* (Penguin Books, 2013), ch. 22.
5. Pirsig, Robert. *Zen and the Art of Motorcycle Maintenance: An Inquiry Into Values.* Reprint ed. (HarperCollins e-books, 2009), ch. 17.
6. Tzu, Lao, and Stephen Mitchell. *Tao Te Ching: A New English Version.* Reprint ed. (Harper Perennial, 2009), ch. 48.

7. Suzuki, Shunryu. *Zen Mind, Beginner's Mind: 50th Anniversary Edition* (Shambhala, 2020), pt. 1 Posture.

8. Watts, Alan, and Chopra Deepak Md. *The Wisdom of Insecurity: A Message for an Age of Anxiety* (Vintage, 2011), ch. 7.

9. Jackson, Phil, and Hugh Delehanty. *Eleven Rings: The Soul of Success*. (Penguin Books, 2013), ch. 4.

10. Chopra, Deepak. *The Seven Spiritual Laws of Success: A Practical Guide to the Fulfillment of Your Dreams*. (Amber-Allen Publishing, 2011), ch. 4.

11. Sadhguru. *Inner Engineering: A Yogi's Guide to Joy*. 1st ed. (Harmony, 2016), pt. 2 No Boundary, No Burden.

12. Krishnamurti, Jiddu, and Mary Lutyens. *Freedom from the Known* (San Francisco: HarperSanFrancisco, 2009), ch. 3.

Chapter Six

1. Tolle, Eckhart. *The Power of Now: A Guide to Spiritual Enlightenment* (Novato: New World Library, 2010), ch. 2.

2. Mooji. *Vaster Than Sky, Greater Than Space: What You Are Before You Became* (Boulder: Sounds True, 2016), ch. 1.

3. Prabhupada, Bhaktivedanta Swami. *Bhagavad-Gita As It Is*. (Bhaktivedanta Book Trust, 1989), ch. 2 Text 20.

4. Tolle, Eckhart. *A New Earth: Awakening to Your Life's Purpose*. Reprint ed. (Penguin, 2006), ch. 10.

Chapter Seven

1. Watts, Alan, and Chopra Deepak Md. *The Wisdom of Insecurity: A Message for an Age of Anxiety* (Vintage, 2011), ch. 3.

2. Balsekar, Ramesh. *Confusion No More: For the Spiritual Seeker*. (Watkins, 2012), ch. Who Cares?.

3. Watts, Alan. *Out of Your Mind: Tricksters, Interdependence, and the Cosmic Game of Hide and Seek*. (Sounds True, 2017), ch. 3.

4. Maharaj, Nisargadatta, and Maurice Frydman. *I Am That*. 2nd American ed. (Durham: The Acorn Press, 2012), ch. 11.

5. Braden, Gregg. *The Divine Matrix: Bridging Time, Space, Miracles, and Belief*. 1st ed. (Hay House Inc., 2008), ch. 1.

6. Luke 17:21 (King James Bible)

7. Suzuki, Shunryu. *Zen Mind, Beginner's Mind: 50th Anniversary Edition* (Shambhala, 2020), Pt. 1 Breathing.

8. Watts, Alan. "Nature of Consciousness," https://alanwatts.org/3-4-8-nature-of-consciousness-part-3/.

9. Maharaj, Nisargadatta, and Maurice Frydman. *I Am That*. 2nd American ed. (Durham: The Acorn Press, 2012), ch. 51.

10. Walsch, Neale Donald. *Conversations with God: An Uncommon Dialogue, Book 1*. 1st ed. (TarcherPerigee, 1996), ch. 1.

11. Tzu, Lao, and Stephen Mitchell. *Tao Te Ching: A New English Version*. Reprint ed. (Harper Perennial, 2009), ch. 42.

12. Watts, Alan. *The Book: On the Taboo Against Knowing Who You Are*. Reissue ed. (Vintage Books, 2011), ch. 1.

13. Tzu, Lao, and Stephen Mitchell. *Tao Te Ching: A New English Version*. Reprint ed. (Harper Perennial, 2009), ch. 56.

14. Sachdeva, Gautam, and Ramesh Balsekar. *Pointers From Ramesh Balsekar*. (Yogi Impressions Books, 2012), Ch. Destiny.

15. Watts, Alan, and Chopra Deepak Md. *The Wisdom of Insecurity: A Message for an Age of Anxiety* (Vintage, 2011), ch. 7.

16. Prabhupada, Bhaktivedanta Swami. *Bhagavad-Gita As It Is*. (Bhaktivedanta Book Trust, 1989), ch. 2 Text 47.

17. Schucman, Helen, and William Thetford. *A Course in Miracles-Original Edition*. Original Edition-1972. (Course in Miracles Society, 2006), Introduction.

18. Carse, David. *Perfect Brilliant Stillness*. First Paperback Ed. (Paragate Publishing, 2005), ch. 27.

19. Adyashanti. *The End of Your World: Uncensored Straight Talk on the Nature of En-*

lightenment. (Sounds True, 2010), ch. 3.

Chapter Eight

1. Watts, Alan, and Chopra Deepak Md. *The Wisdom of Insecurity: A Message for an Age of Anxiety* (Vintage, 2011), Introduction.

2. Maharaj, Nisargadatta, and Maurice Frydman. *I Am That.* 2nd American ed. (Durham: The Acorn Press, 2012), ch. 47.

3. Prabhupada, Bhaktivedanta Swami. *Bhagavad-Gita As It Is.* (Bhaktivedanta Book Trust, 1989), ch. 6 Text 19.

4. Foster, Jeff, and Licata Matt PhD. *Falling in Love with Where You Are: A Year of Prose and Poetry on Radically Opening Up to the Pain and Joy of Life.* Illustrated ed. (Non-Duality, 2013), Nothing is Waiting.

5. Maharaj, Nisargadatta, and Maurice Frydman. *I Am That.* 2nd American ed. (Durham: The Acorn Press, 2012), ch. 81.

6. Tolle, Eckhart. *A New Earth: Awakening to Your Life's Purpose.* Reprint ed. (Penguin, 2006), ch. 2.

7. Hesse, Hermann. *Siddhartha.* 1st ed. (GENERAL PRESS, 2018), ch. GOVINDA.

8. Watts, Alan, and Chopra Deepak Md. *The Wisdom of Insecurity: A Message for an Age of Anxiety* (Vintage, 2011), ch. 1.

9. Spira, Rupert. *Being Aware of Being Aware (The Essence of Meditation Series).* 1st ed.

(Sahaja, 2017), Introduction.

10. Yogananda, Paramhansa. *Autobiography of a Yogi: The Original 1946 Edition.* 2nd ed. (Commerce: Crystal Clarity Publishers, 2005), ch. 43.

11. Suzuki, Shunryu. *Zen Mind, Beginner's Mind: 50th Anniversary Edition* (Shambhala, 2020), pt. 1 Control.

12. Tzu, Lao, and Stephen Mitchell. *Tao Te Ching: A New English Version.* Reprint ed. (Harper Perennial, 2009), ch. 28.

13. Tzu, Lao, and Stephen Mitchell. *Tao Te Ching: A New English Version.* Reprint ed. (Harper Perennial, 2009), ch. 18-19.

Made in the USA
Middletown, DE
19 June 2021

42763708R10156